2/03

D0722684

Ben's Story

Ben's Story

Holocaust Letters with Selections from the Dutch Underground Press

Edited by Kees W. Bolle

Southern Illinois University Press

Carbondale and Edwardsville

Frontispiece: Ben Wessels, 1941 (courtesy of Johan Schipper); pit filled with bodies at the concentration camp of Bergen-Belsen, found when British forces reached the camp April 15, 1945 (courtesy Rijksinstituut voor Oorlogsdocumentatie).

Library of Congress Cataloging-in-Publication Data

Wessels, Benjamin Leo, 1926–1945.
    Ben's story : Holocaust letters with selections from the Dutch underground press / edited by Kees W. Bolle.
        p.   cm.
        1. Wessels, Benjamin Leo, 1926–1945—Correspondence. 2. Jews—Netherlands—Biography. 3. Holocaust, Jewish (1939–1945)—Netherlands—Personal narratives. 4. Schipper, Johan—Correspondence. 5. World War, 1939–1945—Netherlands—Underground literature. I. Bolle, Kees W. II. Title.

    DS135.N6 W528 2001
    940.53′18′092—dc21
                                                    00-059492
    ISBN 0-8093-2374-5 (cloth : alk. paper)

The paper used in this publication meets the minimum requirements of American National Standard for Information Sciences—Permanence of Paper for Printed Library Materials, ANSI Z39.48-1992. ∞

In memory of Ben Wessels

Contents

Illustrations

Preface

This book, which mentally I then called "Letters to Oost-voorne," began as a debt of honor toward a friend of my youth, Ben Wessels, who died a victim in the German concentration camp Bergen-Belsen. The task of translating the letters of this friend and preparing them for publication seemed simple, but it soon grew into a much more encompassing activity. I found that I could not mourn and honor my friend, one Shoah victim among so many, without trying in my way what others have attempted in theirs: I was destined, having taught history for a good many years, to present what happened in a particular manner, which the written legacy itself seemed to demand. My task became to show a certain precise view of the Second World War, without any of the abstraction that generally accompanies historical accounts. The letters of Ben Wessels themselves show the "ordinariness," the obviousness, of events that took place. And this set the goal for the work.

Readers who know me as a historian of religions may be surprised at my undertaking *Ben's Story*. It is never possible to interpret religiohistorical documents in isolation, apart from economics, politics, literature, and so forth. The reverse is also true. Documents without overt reference to religion may, to be fully grasped, require an open eye for religion. Whatever else may be said, the material in *Ben's Story* cannot fail to touch us on the deepest level. And besides, I did not write this material but was enabled to present it through the help of friends and the efforts of the Netherlands Institute for War Documentation.

Although the account presented in this book is unlike most history writing, it is not by chance that I am indebted first of all to a historian: Jacques Klok, archivist of the city of Brielle, the principal city on the island of Voorne in Holland. Not only are the archives under his charge immaculately arranged and preserved, in their range from the prehistoric and medieval and the first glimpse of victory over the Spaniards, to the most recent Delta works, and not only is their location in view of the Catharijnekerk of the old walled city enough to tempt a historian to switch his field of specialty to the southern section of the province of South Holland, I shall remember above all that Jacques Klok's personal assistance was priceless. The help he gave me was that of the chronicler—in the profound sense that Charles Péguy gave the term: one who lives in and witnesses the events that must orient us, if our existence is to make any sense. Among the unexpected documents were his own personal notes on day-to-day events during the war.

Other persons on whom I relied can also be said to share in this chronicling function, without having the trained historian's tendency to explain and play the sovereign lord over the "facts" and "meanings" of their stories. Johan Schipper, the retired school principal of Rockanje, who received and preserved Ben Wessels' letters, filled in many details needed for my understanding. Johan, Ben, and I were playmates and the three youngest musicians in Volharding, the village wind orchestra in Oostvoorne. Of the three of us, Johan was always the one who preserved things, shells, pictures of birds, and other treasures. This book is due to his custodianship. He carefully preserved all of Ben's letters. My sister Leni Bolle, who during the war years was a nurse on the island of Goeree en Overflakkee, to the south of Voorne, clarified my own recollections; and at my request, she traveled with her camera and contacted people whose memories aided and corrected our own. I am grateful also to my other sister, Trien Mos-Bolle, presently living in Maassluis, near The Hague, where at my request she checked and verified some information presented in this book.

For information concerning the Wessels family, I am grateful to P. H. Peper, who knew about things that had to be kept secret and could not be mentioned by Ben in his letters. One most special detail concerned the seemingly miraculous rescue of the youngest member of the Wessels family, Carla. In the midst of horror, there was reason to speak of true miracles, and occasionally, as in this instance, even the greatest miracle of all—a miracle of courage!—did occur. And again, the ordinariness of the miracle is its most striking feature. When Ben Wessels' parents were arrested, an ordinary woman, who happened to help in the household, claimed that Carla was her daughter. That was all the stuff the miracle required.

Without the Netherlands Institute for War Documentation, I could not have gotten my selections from the wartime underground press; these selections form the bulk and the continuity of this book, including several photographs, and constitute much of what was needed for the intended "specific" view of the Second World War. Ellen T. Kaplan has been my great ally once more, correcting my own writing and addressing the treacherous problems of translating the Dutch to which I was too close, having grown up with it during the war years.

I owe a debt of gratitude to Philip Winsor, retired senior editor of Pennsylvania State University Press, who in deep interest and friendship rendered invaluable service in making the manuscript ready for publication, and certainly not in the last place, to James Simmons, the editorial director of Southern Illinois University Press, who did everything possible to facilitate and polish my work in memory of my friend Ben and so many others.

Chronology

The events in this chronology are separated into three categories designated by the indentions.

Political and War Events
>   Anti-Jewish Measures, Concentration Camps, and Resistance
>>   The Wessels Family
>>>   Sept. 29, 1886. Birth of Izaäk Wessels.
>>>   Oct. 25, 1887. Birth of Antje Wessels–van Dijk.
>>>   Apr. 19, 1922. Birth of Nathan Benjamin Wessels.
>>>   Sept. 28, 1926. Birth of Benjamin Leo Wessels.
>>>   Mar. 7, 1929. Birth of Carolina (Carla) Clara Wessels.

1931. Foundation of the NSB (the Nationaal-Socialistische Beweging [Dutch National Socialist], the Dutch Fascist, later Nazistic, political party). Anton Mussert, one of the founders, becomes the "general leader."

1932. Formation of the WA (Weerafdeling, or Weerbaarheidsafdeling), the armed division of the NSB. Dissolved in 1935 as a result of a government interdiction of private militias, reestablished in 1940 after the German occupation of the Netherlands.

Among the most useful reference works for Second World War chronology are (for the Netherlands) A. H. Paape a. o., *Handboek van de tweede wereldoorlog*, 2 vols. (Utrecht-Antwerpen: Het Spectrum, 1983); (general) Marcel Baudot a. o., translated from the French by Alvin D. Coox and Thomas R. H. Havens, *The Historical Encyclopedia of World War II* (New York: Greenwich House, 1977); and Louis L. Snyder, *Encyclopedia of the Third Reich* (New York: Paragon House, 1989); the last, first published in 1976, contains an excellent bibliography.

Aug. 1–16, 1936. Olympic Games are held in Berlin. In boxing, Joe Louis beats the German champion Max Schmeling. To many, the victory of a black man over the Germanic hero signals a victory over National Socialist racism.

Jan. 30, 1937. Hitler promises to respect Belgium's neutrality.

Apr. 24, 1937. German planes bomb Guernica in northwestern Spain, the Basque region. This event, lent fame through one of Pablo Picasso's paintings, was one of the acts by the Axis Powers (Germany and Italy) aiding Francisco Franco to transform Spain into a fascist nation.

> July 1, 1937. Pastor Martin Niemöller, U-boat captain in the First World War, now one of the great names in the German Confessing Church (opposed to the National Socialist policies), is arrested.

Mar. 12, 1938. German troops invade Austria, resulting on the next day in the official Anschluss (euphemism for annexation by Germany) of Austria.

Sept. 29, 1938. Munich Conference of Adolf Hitler, Neville Chamberlain (prime minister of Britain), and Édouard Daladier (prime minister of France), giving Hitler a free hand in annexing Sudetenland, part of Czechoslovakia.

Nov. 9, 1938. Kristallnacht (Crystal Night). Violence perpetrated against Jews in cities throughout Germany.

> Jan. 24, 1939. Hermann Goering (founder of the Gestapo, Secret State Police) orders S. Heidrich (chief of the Sipo, i.e. Sicherheitspolizei, the Security Police) to find a "solution for the Jewish question through emigration or evacuation."

Jan. 26, 1939. Aided by Italian troops, Franco conquers Barcelona.

> Jan. 30, 1939. Reichstag speech by Hitler, in which he declares that in a new war the Jews of Europe will be eradicated.

> Feb. 13, 1939. The cabinet of the Netherlands government decides to build a camp for refugees from Germany: this is the beginning of Westerbork, later transformed into a transition camp for Jews by the Germans. (The camp of Vught in the south of the country was built as a concentration camp by the Germans.)

Mar. 15, 1939. German surprise attack on Czechoslovakia, in violation of the pact of Munich.

Mar. 28, 1939. The nationalists—the party of Franco—occupy Madrid. Three days later, Spain's Civil War comes to an end with the occupation of the remaining cities that had resisted Franco.

June 20, 1939. First test flight of a rocket plane in Germany (the Heinkel 176).

July 26, 1939. The Zentralstelle für jüdische Auswanderung (Center for Jewish Emigration) established in Prague by Adolf Eichmann.

Aug. 28, 1939. Test flight of the first jet plane: the Heinkel 178.

Sept. 1, 1939. Germany attacks Poland: beginning of the Second World War.

> On this same day, Hitler gives his euthanasia order: five special establishments are to kill the insane. Some eighty thousand incurable mental patients are killed. Limits are set only in 1941 after church protests.

Oct. 6, 1939. Final capitulation of Polish troops.

Apr. 9, 1940. Germany invades Denmark and Norway. Denmark capitulates the same day. Norwegian troops lay down arms on June 10.

Friday, May 10, 1940. Germany invades the Netherlands, Belgium, and Luxembourg. Winston Churchill becomes prime minister of Britain's war cabinet.

Wednesday, May 15, 1940. Capitulation of the Netherlands.

May 29, 1940. Inaugural address of Dr. Arthur Seyss-Inquart, Reichskommissar für die besetzten niederländischen Gebiete (commissar of the Reich for the occupied Dutch territories). He promises to respect the rights of the citizens of the Netherlands.

> End of May 1940. Johann (Hanns) Baptist Albin Rauter, like Seyss-Inquart an Austrian by birth, is appointed Generalkommissar für das Sicherheitswesen and Höhere SS- und Polizeiführer in the occupied Netherlands. This means he became chief of the SS and other German security forces in the country. Though formally subordinate to Seyss-Inquart, Rauter was in fact answerable only to Heinrich Himmler, the chief commander of the SS, to whom he was devoted. In the

First World War, he was an officer in the Austro-Hungarian army. After that war, he led an adventurous life in various ultrarightist militias zealous for the "great-German" cause, against Poles, Yugoslavs, and above all against communists. He had been wounded more than once and would be severely wounded once more during his career in the Netherlands.

June 1, 1940. Jews are forbidden any role in the air-raid protection services.

June 14, 1940. German troops occupy Paris.

July 4, 1940. Ordinance of Seyss-Inquart: listening to a number of foreign radio stations is prohibited.

Aug. 31, 1940 (the birthday of Queen Wilhelmina). Publication of the first issue of *Vrij Nederland* (the free Netherlands), one of the first among the most widely distributed papers of the underground press.

Oct. 4, 1940. All employees in official functions are asked to sign an "Aryan declaration" (i.e., principally a statement to indicate their non-Jewishness, also aimed at excluding Gypsies and nonwhites).

Oct. 24, 1940. Official protest of the principal Protestant churches in the Netherlands addressed to Seyss-Inquart against the repudiation of Jewish officials.

Nov. 25–26, 1940. Student protests at Leiden University and the Technical School of Delft against the dismissal of Jewish professors, judges, teachers, and other officials. The next day, Nov. 27, both institutions are shut down.

Jan. 10, 1941. Ordinance of Seyss-Inquart requiring registration of "all persons partly or wholly of Jewish blood."

Feb. 10, 1941. First issue of *Het Parool,* widely read underground newspaper.

Feb. 11–12, 1941. Seyss-Inquart's delegate in Amsterdam gives the order to seal off the old Jewish quarter of the city. (Though this section of the city had assembled a large percentage of Jews among its population, the city never had a "ghetto.")

Feb. 13, 1941. Through the services of the newly formed Jewish Council, the Jews of Amsterdam are ordered to hand in any weapons they may have.

Feb. 25–26, 1941. "The February Strike." In Feb. 1941, the WA, the military branch of the Dutch NSB, were given a free hand in anti-Jewish actions in the Jewish quarter of Amsterdam. Inhabitants, not only in the immediate area the WA had singled out for their violence but also from other parts of the city, resisted with force. Battles between the WA and the city's fighting men ensued on Feb. 19; a member of the WA was killed. Thereupon the Ordnungspolizei (Grüne Polizei, the Green Police) stepped in. *Razzias* (see introduction) on Feb. 22–23 led to the arrest of more than four hundred Jews. (They were all sent to the German concentration camps Buchenwald and Mauthausen; only one of them survived.) Immediately after the first *razzia,* the CPN (the Communist Party, then illegal) and the Derde Front (a revolutionary socialist organization) initiated the plan for a strike. The strike was an immediate and overwhelming success, indeed general, and spontaneously accepted by the population. It was a mass protest against the Germans and the NSB. Originating and centered in Amsterdam, it sparked strikes elsewhere and took the Germans by surprise. They reacted with many more arrests and with executions. (The Dutch commemorate the event annually and take pride in the February Strike as the first and only instance where a city rebelled against a pogrom.)

May 15, 1941. Distribution of identity cards begins in the Netherlands. The population is ordered to hand in certain metals. Around this time, several sections of railway track are closed to public use in order to facilitate the transportation of German soldiers to the Russian front. Also in the month of May 1941, obligatory labor service is announced in the Netherlands for all men aged 18–35.

Sunday, June 22, 1941. Germany begins its war with Russia. The news arrives, is passed on, and causes a stir even on the crowded beaches. The feeling that this spells the beginning of the end for Germany is widespread, but the Germans will do reasonably well in their campaign until the winter of 1941–42. That winter would turn out to be very severe in every part of Europe, including the Netherlands. That same winter would bring a definitive end to the blitzkrieg, the lightninglike war the Germans conducted and were so proud of. And by then, the Royal Air Force (RAF) would have put an end to all serious German plans for an attack on England. Nevertheless, during the summer of 1941, the crowds on the beach, obviously still able to enjoy themselves, had no more idea of the suffering that still lay ahead than did Izaäk Wessels.

Aug. 1941. Beginning in August, Jews are no longer allowed to attend school with non-Jews.

Nov. 1941. In Africa, the last Italian troops surrender to the British at Gondar (in Ethiopia). Even earlier in the year, Emperor Haile Selassie had been able to return to the capital, Addis Ababa. After the successes the Italians had scored in July 1940, taking Kassala in the Sudan and overrunning British Somaliland, the British victories, though far away, were additional encouraging signs, indicating weaknesses in the Axis. (The English were supported by Australian and South African forces.)

Dec. 7, 1941. The Japanese attack Pearl Harbor.

Dec. 11, 1941. Germany and Italy declare war on the United States.

Jan. 20, 1942. Wannsee Conference. Conference held at Wannsee, near Berlin, by order of Reinhard Heydrich, SS-Obergruppenführer and General der Polizei, supreme commander of SS and German secret police, hence central in the execution of anti-Jewish measures. The meeting was presided over by Adolf Eichmann and attended by fourteen government officials. The attendants were told of the decision to "evacuate" eleven million European Jews toward the east. This meeting was crucial for the "final solution of the Jewish question." *Evacuation* implied systematic deportation and destruction.

Apr.–May 1942. The yellow star is introduced. Jews are ordered to wear the yellow Star of David on their clothes in public. Beginning May 2, Jews in the Netherlands are obliged to wear it. In Germany, this method of marking and humiliating the Jews had begun officially in Sept. 1941. Even earlier, after the Germans had overrun Poland (Sept. 1939), Nazis had introduced the yellow star there but in a rather erratic fashion, with different designs for the hated marking (Presser, *Ondergang*, 1:219). In Amsterdam, on Apr. 29, 1942, the chairmen of the Jewish Council were summoned to appear in the office of SS-Hauptsturmführer Aus der Fünten and notified of the new rules. The star was to be six-pointed, outlined in black, its size like the palm of a hand, and, in black lettering, the word *Jood* (Jew) written on it. The star was to be sewn to the garment and to be clearly visible on the left side of the chest. An additional rule forbade Jews to wear any decorations or badges of honor. We have information from the minutes written by an SS-Hauptsturmführer in the office that the chairmen, A. Asscher and D. Cohen, were dumbfounded by the latest German measure. Pulling themselves together, they assured Aus der Fünten "that it was no pleasant message for Jewry, but that they personally would be proud to wear it and thereby become honorary citizens of the Netherlands." The same report mentions that at that very occasion the stars were made available and that the number of them was 569,355 (Presser, *Ondergang*, 1:221, who notes that the number of ready-made stars is puzzling).

> Aug. 14, 1942. Nathan Benjamin Wessels deported from Oostvoorne.

> Aug. 17, 1942. Nan Wessels leaves on a transport from Westerbork for an unknown destination.

> Sept. 1942. Death of Nan Wessels, most probably in Auschwitz. (The population register in Westvoorne gives Sept. 30 as the date.)

> Sept. 26, 1942. Deportation of all remaining Jews from Oostvoorne: the families Wessels and van Dijk.

> 1943. The house in Oostvoorne in which the Wessels lived (and which was owned by a relative of Antje Wessels–van Dijk) is "taken over" by the Niederländische Grundstücksverwaltung, the German organization for "Dutch real estate management."

Jan. 15, 1943. Concentration camp Vught put to use for the first time.

Jan. 26, 1943. All twelve hundred patients of the Jewish mental hospital Het Apeldoornse Bos are loaded in baggage wagons and transported across the border. No one heard from them again. Similar measures are taken in nursing homes in The Hague in the following month.

End of Jan. 1943. The first issue of *Trouw* appears (not in Amsterdam but in Meppel, in the eastern Netherlands).

Feb. 6, 1943. The Dutch churches write their letter of protest to Seyss-Inquart. The following weekend, on Sunday, Feb. 21, it is read in the churches.

May 1943. Destruction of thirty-eight U-boats. The situation in the Atlantic turns in favor of the Allied forces.

May 15, 1943. Rauter announces that all radios must be handed in.

July 1943. Having witnessed a launching test, Hitler orders priority development of the V-2. (The V-2 was far superior to its predecessor in speed, altitude, and guiding system, and is considered a real predecessor to the Inter-Continental Ballistic Missile class. One of its principal engineers was Wernher von Braun.)

Approximately Aug. 15, 1943. Arrest and deportation of Izaäk Wessels and Antje Wessels–van Dijk to Westerbork.

Aug. 24, 1943. Izaäk and Antje Wessels put on transport from Westerbork to Auschwitz.

Aug. 27, 1943. Death of Izaäk and Antje Wessels in Auschwitz.

Late Sept. or Early Oct. 1943. Deportation of Benjamin Wessels to Westerbork.

1944. The Wessels house in Oostvoorne is sold to a man from a nearby village.

Jan. 1, 1944. The Russians, pursuing the German armies, enter Poland.

Feb. 19–24, 1944. Heavy Allied bombing attacks on Germany's industrial centers for the production of airplanes. In this action, the Germans lose more than five hundred fighter planes.

Apr. 11, 1944. A precision bombardment by the British RAF destroys the central registry of population in The Hague. This loss was serious for the Germans' ability to locate people for their purposes.

> Spring 1944. Transport of Benjamin Wessels to Bergen-Belsen.

June 6, 1944. Invasion in Normandy begins.

June 13, 1944. Beginning of V-1 attacks on London.

Sept. 5, 1944. Dolle Dinsdag (Mad Tuesday). The Germans had been defeated in Normandy and had not yet been able to reorganize their defenses. Belgium, to the south of the Netherlands, had been liberated quickly. In this situation, and probably triggered by an optimistic Dutch broadcast from radio London, on this Mad Tuesday, euphoria pervaded the country. Many believed that Allied soldiers had already crossed the large rivers in the center of the Netherlands. A number of NSB fled to Germany. Especially in hindsight, the term *mad* is appropriate. The western part of the country (including Holland proper, distinct from the eastern provinces) was still to experience its worst winter of hunger and terror under occupation.

> Sept. 3, 1944. The final (seventy-sixth) transport leaves from Westerbork to Auschwitz.

Sept. 8, 1944. The first V-2 offensive against British territory begins, with a missile launched from The Hague.

Sept. 11, 1944. Patrols of the British Second Division cross the Dutch-Belgian border into the Dutch province of Limburg. From Luxembourg, American troops enter Germany.

> Jan. 27, 1945. Soviet forces liberate Auschwitz.

Mar. 6, 1945. Resistance fighters attack, fail to kill, but severely wound the German SS general Rauter.

> Mar. 22, 1945. Benjamin Leo Wessels dies in Bergen-Belsen.

Mar. 29, 1945. The last German missile, a V-1, is launched toward England but is shot down before reaching its goal.

> Apr. 15, 1945. British forces liberate Bergen-Belsen.

Apr. 30, 1945. Soldiers of the Red Army plant their flag on the German Reichstag Building in Berlin.

May 4, 1945. All German forces in the Netherlands, northwest Germany, Denmark, Helgoland, and the Frisian Islands agree to capitulate. The capitulation takes effect on May 5, at 8:00 A.M.

May 7, 1945. Unconditional surrender of all remaining German forces signed in Reims by the German general Alfred Jodl as head of the chiefs of staff.

Nov. 20, 1945–Aug. 31, 1946. The Nuremberg Trials. Jodl, Seyss-Inquart, and others are hanged.

1949. As part of the nationwide restoration of rights, ownership of the Wessels house is returned to the prewar owner's widow.

Mar. 25, 1949. Execution of Rauter, who had been extradited to the Netherlands and there put on trial. Rauter, the chief commander of the SS and other German security forces, was held responsible for the reign of terror.

Ben's Story

Introduction

Portrayal of the Second World War

The further back we look in history, the more events become "items," each of them clearly visible, all by itself. Thus we may come to see Caesar invading Gaul or Hannibal struggling over the Alps with his elephants. We know in principle that such isolated images are distortions, and yet our minds easily accept them, and most textbook history accounts leave such residues in our collective memory.

The Second World War came to an end more than half a century ago. We have reached a time in which people think of the Second World War as one homogeneous topic. Even when we refer to it in irony as "the last good war," we realize the tendency to sum it up in one image.

Distortion is worse in this case than in other cases. Not only was there nothing homogeneous about the Second World War but storing it in our memory as one "object" next to others amounts to a deception about ourselves. The Second World War shaped the twentieth century, and it has shaped us. Regardless of whether we are "survivors," all of us in this postwar world have become inured to cruelty, violence, and the massive misuse of language. Such simple facts alert me, and surely should alert you, that the Second World War refuses to be summed up by our intellect.

This book is an attempt to narrate firsthand, without homogenizing, without commentary that polishes, what happened in the

Netherlands under German occupation. How can there be a first-hand account? To begin with, we have the underground press of the Netherlands, publications and items of information collected, written, and distributed by men and women who exposed themselves to death by acting as they did. Then we have a group of letters from a Jewish boy who grew to be a man and died in a German concentration camp. Together, both the news and reflections in the underground press in all their variety and the experiences of the boy give us an unmediated, direct portrayal.

The focus of attention in the story of Jews in the Netherlands during the Second World War is generally the city of Amsterdam. In this book, too, Amsterdam is the center, but there is a difference. My grade school friend Ben Wessels, wearer of the yellow star, addresses his letters to another of my friends, Johan Schipper, in the village of Oostvoorne on the North Sea—inhabited at the time by no more than some three thousand souls. And though Amsterdam is the scene of the action, not all misery relates to it: for many who had not lived in Amsterdam before misfortune brought them there, the focus of thought, the ties with friends, the hope of returning centered on such villages as Oostvoorne. The sharpness of this focus, so visible in Ben Wessels' letters, is worth preserving within the massive array of larger facts and events because the experience of individuals is indispensable for an attempt at understanding.

The plight of European Jews, the attempt made by Hitler's Germany to exterminate them, has yielded a vast literature.[1] A host of scholars in the study of man and human nature have descended on it, on the bulk, the complexity, the horror of its documents.

The Nazis were not the originators of racial discrimination, nor of torture and death inflicted on a group singled out from the rest, and there is no scholarly disagreement on cruelty as an exceedingly ancient characteristic of the human race. From all we know and can infer, Cro-Magnon man may have had an active part in decimating *Homo heidelbergensis*. Yet the Second World War is a watershed; cruelty, torture, persecution for political ideology; illusory, pathologically conjured-up, pitilessly enforced divisions of the world into a "we" and a "they," with a violent front separating the two: all these have become standard, reflected, for example, in the world's newspapers, since Hitler's uncanny power reached its zenith. The Germans have the unenviable place in history of having enthroned the Nazis; but the Nazis' deliberate and massive onslaught on human lives has become the special mark of our age.

We simply cannot get around the *official and institutional* antihuman measures that pervade the world we take for granted. And while the historian, the human being, the friend of a victim, can prophesy or exclaim, hoping to be heard, no hope of change exists if we cannot imagine the fate of individuals in such mass misery. I would like Ben Wessels' letters to contribute to the fostering of that imagination. For if one Salvadoran was forced from the United States back to his country, frantic that torture might await him, we have a case like Ben's. If one Haitian looked to the United States in vain for refuge from a ruthless regime, we have a case like Ben's. If one Surinamer migrating to Holland was placed last in line by the Immigration Police, we have a case like Ben's.

Ben Wessels' letters do not express an abundance of agony — though agony is certainly present. The final, censored messages from the transition camp of Westerbork in the eastern Netherlands and the very last postcard from Bergen-Belsen do not even attempt to express the reality of the situation. In only one letter, after the disappearance of his parents, does the young writer lament outright (August 19, 1943). But throughout his letters, we hear his nostalgia, his longing for his village.

What is more natural than the longing for one's own village? This material is hardly startling. Yet it is just these very natural and essential ingredients of all human life that disappear in our comprehension of "history." The point is not negligible. We speak too easily of such things as "the destruction of European Jewry." Our abstractions blot out the lesson that not only were there individual people wreaking the destruction but also there were ordinary individuals, belonging to specific places, not mere elements making up Jewry and Judaism, who were the victims.

The point is made by Jean Améry, a Jew from Austria who found his way to Belgium and became involved in the Belgian resistance.

An SS man, housed in the same building where Améry was noisily carrying on with his comrades, knocked at the door one day. Améry opened the door to him and, he tells us, after the initial shock at the sight of the SS insignia, found himself moved most of all by the speech of the man, for it was the dialect of the very region of Austria from which Améry himself had come. For a moment, his nostalgia almost won out over his fear.[2] ("Odd, isn't it," Ben Wessels writes on August 7, 1943, "that one can long so much for a village.")

Most normally, most unphilosophically, Ben's letters express this ordinary belonging that typifies not abstractions but our existence, and not existence in general but that sort of specific existence that indeed gets destroyed when destruction occurs. Ben never had in mind a reading public, and yet his letters express soberly and starkly the ordinary level, the common life cells in which the most incisive and cruel human transformation occurred in our century. The little facts of Ben's concern, including the scarcity of shoelaces, the incalculable value of a flashlight battery, and his desire for the musical instrument he used to play, tell a story that shows us some of the bare bones of suffering in the Second World War.

Ben Wessels was born September 28, 1926, in Oostvoorne and died in Bergen-Belsen on March 22, 1945, less than a month before the English liberated the camp. The Red Cross report on his death is scant; but of course our general knowledge of Bergen-Belsen by the end of the war suggests what the end must have been like. The camp had become overcrowded with prisoners moved from camps elsewhere as the Russians came closer to German territory, and famine and contagious diseases ravaged it.

Ben Wessels, Johan Schipper, to whom almost all the letters are addressed, and I were friends in our grammar school days. Ben and I were classmates at the public school in the center of the village, and Johan attended a private school on the outskirts, where I also had gone before my family moved close to the center. Shortly after the war began, we parted for different high schools in different towns on the island of Voorne; Johan and Ben went to one, I to the other. However, Ben joined the wind orchestra, which Johan and I played in, and we met at the weekly rehearsals. Johan carefully preserved the letters Ben wrote after his forced departure, and these form part of the substance of this book.

It may seem strange that so many years went by before anyone looked closely at the documents of what happened then in our village and with our friends. Again, human facts provide the answers. Joy at the end of the war was so great as to obliterate many miseries and painful memories. Also there is such a thing as historical imagination, which is more, much more, than historical generalizations or statistics and needs time to develop. In the many documents produced immediately after the war, what one finds is less than mediocre, not so much because people tried to justify themselves but because the writers were not yet able to raise questions, or to see proportions in the events that had rolled over them and dragged them along. At the time, it seemed as if there were only heroes and victims, proud victors and properly punished evildoers. The historical imagination that sees and distinguishes needs time, must mature, and has to drink from the wells of compassion. Above all, the detection of the human elements of which all history is made is an ability that can be nurtured only very slowly.

I have transcribed and translated the texts that were so fortunately kept in a safe drawer by Johan Schipper. Wherever explanation seemed needed, I have provided some commentary. A few photographs help the reader to visualize the scenes in the village, in Amsterdam, and in the camp of Westerbork, hence to visualize the places where Ben resided successively.

After the preface to this volume, I have provided a chronology of events related to the war, to the Jews, and to the Wessels family. Ben's letters themselves are accompanied by translated excerpts from the underground press in the Netherlands. The passages from these newspapers, which were strictly illegal and whose editors, when found out, suffered severe losses or death, form the natural context for and elucidation of the letters. However, it may be helpful to present here the most general line of development we see in the letters.

Soon after the Germans occupied the Netherlands, anti-Jewish measures were taken, yet their anti-Jewish nature was not evident at once. The institution of personal identity papers seemed fairly harmless, and the appearance of the letter *J* on the identity document of a Jew appeared odd rather than dangerous. Only gradually did ugly effects become visible. More and more rules made employment of Jewish officials, teachers, artists, and so on impossible. In the summer of 1942, the first steps toward deportations began. The existing traditions of officialdom, the precise registration of the population, the Jewish Councils newly established at the instigation of the German authorities and made up of prominent members in Dutch national life, all formed a willy-nilly yet ready instrumentation for the SS. In August 1942, Nan (Nathan), Ben's older brother, responded to a written summons. Born April 19, 1922, he and many others in his age group were forced to report earlier than the others. He was to report in Rotterdam, and with many others, he did. After his departure, his relatives did not receive even one single message from him. Records uncovered after the war, hence after his death and after the deaths of his parents and his brother, Ben, show that Nan was transported from Westerbork on August 17, 1942; no one is altogether certain of his destination and the place of his death—although in all likelihood it was Auschwitz. The only member of the family who would survive the war was Ben's younger sister, Carla. Carla was mentally retarded and, as a ten-year-old in 1939, before the war, had been entrusted to a nursing home in Hilversum; later, she was moved to a home in Apeldoorn, and then to Amersfoort.[3] When the German measures to round up Jews took effect, the Wessels family declined to accept help and go into hiding.[4] Izaäk Wessels, insisting that he was not guilty of anything, felt that no wrong would come to them. (On this issue, see also the introductory notes to the underground press selections.) In October 1942, Ben and his family were taken from Oostvoorne to Amsterdam, where eventually Carla joined them. (Ben's letters indicate that she arrived but do not provide the exact date or how she was brought to them.) In the German plans for the Netherlands, Amsterdam functioned as the principal collection point for Jews. From there, deportation began in transports and with selections that were for the most part random and, of course, always frightening and that were, especially in the final period of 1943 and 1944, the result of *razzias*. *Razzias* were the SS-led procedures whereby a section of the city was surrounded, cordoned off, and combed for Jewish occupants and other "undesirables." Those caught were sent east, first to Westerbork, the transit camp in Drente, a province bordering Germany, and from there to the camps in Germany and Poland. Ben's parents, Izaäk Wessels and Antje Wessels–van Dijk, were deported on August 24, 1943, going from Westerbork to Auschwitz. The time of their death is unknown.

The only survivor of the Wessels family, as I have said, is Carla, who was three years younger than Ben. She lives now in a home for the mentally handicapped in the central Netherlands. She was born with her handicap, and her escape from the tragic lot of her relatives happened thus: a woman who helped Antje Wessels with her household chores in Amsterdam and who herself was not Jewish claimed that Carla was her child when the house was raided and Izaäk and Antje Wessels both were taken away. This same Carla who survived, and from whom no one expected any of the things for which humankind is praised, is the one person related to the whole history of this book who is now happy, indeed who speaks of her parents and brothers as having left for a little while, to return at any moment.

Almost all of Ben's letters were written in Amsterdam, the dumping ground for Jews before "further transportation." In one of the last letters from Amsterdam, Ben sees the sun setting in the west, and in his thoughts, it is setting right over Oostvoorne, his village on the sea.

Ben's letters show things sometimes by not mentioning them or by mentioning them only inadequately: such was the caution necessary and silently applied at the time, not so much out of political sagacity as out of unreasoned fear. His departure from the village was dreadful. He and his father were dragged before the Ortskommandant, frisked, and robbed by that commander's soldiers. None of these men, including the Kommandant, had any affiliation with the SS or with any of the official Nazi ideologues singled out for blame after the war and made into public scapegoats for all the evil perpetrated in those vicious days. The reality of the experienced cruelty was indeed very different from the distant and distorted understanding that became popularized afterward in America. The evildoers Ben and his father were first subjected to were members of the ordinary infantry, the Wehrmacht, who until that day had been polite customers in the jewelry-and-watch shop of Ben's father. The world had turned upside down overnight. After a horrible introduction into the "dump" of Amsterdam, Ben first writes about the event obliquely. A couple of days later, when things seem more settled, he mentions a bit more, yet without really giving details. Secrecy, fear of the censor, is the order of the day. He is happy to be with his parents, yet at the same time a recurrent, very worried note is struck when he speaks of his older brother. Ben did not live to see the doleful, incomplete Red Cross message that Johan found when he inquired about the family's fate, telling that Nan had been deported from Westerbork for an unknown destination. There is little doubt that Nan, with many, many young people selected for an early call, met his death before the end of 1942. The population register of Oostvoorne, completed after the war, lists Auschwitz as the place of death, but there is no verifiable fact on which this listing rests; we only know that most Jews from the Netherlands were deported to Auschwitz at the time: many of the first large deportations from western Europe in the spring and summer of 1942 ended there. Early on, the "unknown destination" of some was Mauthausen, the infamous camp with its "deathtrap stairs," rocks on a steep slope where inmates were chased down and massacred.[5] However, the population register has the general statistics to support its surmise about Auschwitz.[6] This camp had already been transformed into an extermination camp by January 1942.

Ben's letters are by no means filled up with horror stories. He is growing from boy to man, and his youth is evident many times over. We find him teasing Johan about a girlfriend—for at that time, any intimation of a love affair was surrounded by secretiveness and teasing. Ben's resilience shows in his adaptation to the daily hardships and risks in Amsterdam, especially the fearful *razzias*. He calls them *hardloopwedstrijden*, "running matches," a most ironic euphemism for the SS hunting parties, not infrequently made even worse by blackshirted Dutch Nazi accomplices and some Dutch policemen. Running was not uncommon then, even under "normal" circumstances for Ben: at the time, he was employed as an errand boy by the Jewish Council, whose services the Germans used in their deportation program. Irony to a higher degree, one that he did not need to point out while writing about it, occurs when he finds himself employed as an elevator operator for the Grüne Polizei, often a most dreadful arm of German oppression. Ben shows his age, his resilience, most markedly when early on in the correspondence he begins to *play* the secretiveness called for by the fear of censors and traitors, and to do so with a playfulness that could not serve a practical purpose. It is done as in the game cowboys and Indians or as in detective stories. He changes his signature from the familiar "Ben" or "B. L. Wessels" into "Piet Zeldenrust." The new name sounds common enough in Dutch, yet for all its playfulness, even here a literal meaning of "Zeldenrust" is painfully transparent: "seldom rest" or "hardly ever peaceful."

The period of almost childish playfulness in Amsterdam is brief. The letter of August 19, 1943, reports that Ben's parents have been put on a transport. He now finds himself alone in the city. Shortly thereafter, it is his turn. The busy correspondence soon becomes a trickle, requests for food and clothes and shoes, from the transition camp Westerbork in the eastern part of the Netherlands, then a long period of silence, and finally a postcard from Bergen-Belsen, written in German, in conformity with the regulations. The final postscripts, though unlike the German rules and decrees, sadly take us back to the world of officialdom: they are the responses to Johan's inquiries concerning the Wessels family. Among them is the report on Ben's death in Bergen-Belsen on March 22, 1945, less than six months after his eighteenth birthday.

The Underground Press

By definition, the "underground press" was illegal in the five years the Germans occupied the Netherlands. Underground publication began almost as soon as the country capitulated, on May 15, 1940. In the years that followed, it gave voice to the widest spectrum of opinions, all of them one in their reaction to the German oppressor.

Historians owe the present documentation of the Dutch underground press principally to the Netherlands Institute for War Documentation. Thanks to the tireless employees of that office, we have available on microfiche the reproductions of a great number of illegal papers. The mere act of being in possession of any of these papers was terribly dangerous at the time. Now, at our convenience, we can thumb through more than twelve hundred of them, finding eyewitness accounts, essays, poems, parodies, sermons, rousing political speeches, calls for resistance, and other utterances of an astounding variety. Of course, we must place ourselves back in a time without photocopiers or electronic communication. Most of the archived material was typed and then dittoed, and each piece of equipment, each writer and deliverer in the secret network, was vulnerable in the extreme. Nevertheless, especially when the war began to last longer than anyone had expected, the German pressure and relentless persecution could not overcome that press with its insistence on freedom. Indeed, the measures taken by the Germans seem often to have stimulated growth and inventiveness, and some of the major illegal papers (among them *Het Parool*, *Trouw*, and *De Waarheid*) continued to appear in print throughout the war.

The use I have made of the Dutch underground press—which was more extensive and of greater significance than those in any of the other occupied lands[7]—is naturally limited to only a small selection. My choices were in the first place guided by what Ben Wessels wrote in his letters to his friend Johan Schipper in Oostvoorne. Reactions in the underground press to events from day to day form a natural introduction to, commentary on, and context for Ben's letters. After his last postcard, from Bergen-Belsen, underground press selections provide an epilogue and take us to the end of the war. I have chosen, in particular, passages that reported and discussed the persecution and the fate of the Jews, including sundry cruel treatments, and descriptions of concentration camps. Such reports and discussions were being published well before Ben's forced journey from his village began, and they grew in precision during the time of his stay in the artificial ghetto the Germans created in Amsterdam.

There is, however, a second concern that influenced my process of selection. I have tried to give the reader an idea of the general course of the war—or of wartime—within the perspective of the Netherlands. It is one of those cases in which original documents themselves provide a record about which the historian can certainly write but on which he can hardly improve. We receive a firsthand account of the Second World War from voices that continue to ring true. They fulminate against manifold evils that have not subsided since then — indeed, that have often gained in vehemence: above all, racism, hypocrisy, and not least the fear of acting when human life and justice demand acts. The freedom fighters who were worthy of that name before it became widely used and found in the mouths of politicians, and who wrote in the underground press, were scarcely as upset by anything as by the many who thought of themselves as being "on the good side" but who had nothing at heart except their own safety.

This holy indignation on the part of the underground press seems to me to demand the utmost attention. Perhaps it is an issue that is not in focus in many of our lives, coming vaguely to the surface now and then when we hear about a victim abused, assaulted, murdered, while onlookers did not lift a hand. It would seem that we need extreme examples just to catch a passing glimpse of the matter. We, who live free from the mortal pressures of wartime, do not normally find ourselves in a position where the absolute evil of indifference stares us in the face. Reading the clandestine press of the Second World War, we meet people who experienced a revelation of the wide distribution of this evil. We find exhortations to cowards and condemnations of selfishness.

Throughout the underground press, burning questions are posed: How is it possible that we did not see? In the first article among the present selections, the writer asks: How were we so stupid as to sign the "Aryan declaration"? — for that was one of the stratagems that made perfect registration possible and prepared the way for the transport and murder of Jews. And is it too late? Can we stop the further encroachment of this horror? But later papers make quite clear that resisting is an act of will that becomes the portion of only a few. The writers before us continue to exhort the majority, who think, "It will last out my time. . . ."

The great revelation to the fighters, who found themselves engaged in a struggle for which nothing had prepared them, might also be described as the painful discovery that as a rule people lack *imagination.* The ability to imagine the suffering of others is humanly as necessary as bread, and yet it is dealt out sparsely. It has little to do with education. (Here the underground press shows a thing or two.) Without such imagination, our eyes are not opened to the perversion of justice.

Considering that any work for illegal publications meant risking one's life, the accuracy of detail in the underground press becomes quite amazing. I do not know how many editors of illegal papers met their death. *Trouw* lost virtually its entire editorial staff more than once, and yet each time there were others who took up their places and resurrected the publication, gathering information, reflecting, and writing.

An inevitable question arises: Since so much was written, why didn't people learn what was about to befall them, most especially the Jews, and hide or flee? The answers to this question often concern simple things. For example, straightforward information often is not paid enough attention, for "simple information" is hardly ever as convincing or as acceptable or even as discernible as one might assume. The extermination of Jews has understandably become central in discussions of the Nazi era. As a result, our hindsight tends to overlook the fact that very many things were going on at the same time, and the gruesome activity of exterminating entire groups of people could not command the full vigilance of harassed individuals. I have purposely included passages from underground papers that convey an image of the manifold discontents and threats in day-to-day life under German occupation.[8] Another simple matter that escapes our hindsight is that no one expected the war to go on for as long as it did. The tone is quite audible in Ben's letters and in an occasional added note from his father. In the first couple of years of the war, educated people seemed united in their conviction that a modern war could not last as long as the First World War had lasted.

These very simple facts of history go a long way toward explaining why people, such as Ben Wessels and his family, did not do everything possible to escape or hide before the measures of the Nazis would uproot them. Then, too, when people in the village of Oostvoorne had in fact offered to hide the Wessels family, Izaäk Wessels responded: "We have not done anything wrong, have we?" The unbelief on the side of the burgher that inhuman acts such as those of the SS could occur at all is also a fact of history, and no doubt it was a great weak spot in the defense of Europe.

Historical fact, it is true, shows that in the 1930s, years before the war broke out, the established press had written of harassment and persecutions and regime-instigated murder in Germany. But in the Netherlands, these reports appeared most extensively in publications of the political left: those of the Communists and the Democratic Socialists. The political left had no part in the Netherlands government at that time, and their reports were not given the wide distribution that might have made them effective in the formation of public opinion.

The beginning of the occupation changed the situation dramatically. The first underground paper was published in that same month of May 1940, when the German war machine rolled over Holland; and in the years that followed, illegal papers came off the presses and were cranked out by stencil machines and copied by hand by the thousands. All of them, from whatever political persuasion, reported on the German atrocities. And as I have said, the Dutch underground press as a whole produced more than any other European nation under the German heel.

The writers represented a wide spectrum of political belief. The right and the left, or the former right and the former left, now felt the same oppression and reported the same gruesome events, even if their interpretations differed. These differences were as nothing compared to the differences before the war.

Nevertheless, in spite of all the information that was being made available, not enough was truly known, truly believed, disseminated soon enough and widely enough. The hazy and treacherous entity known as "ideology" played its part. Ideology cannot be measured statistically, but it must be taken very seriously, for it can have a terrible collaborative force in murder and in the submission to degrading acts. The lack of full information in a "free" press before the war was in part due to an intention to remain neutral, as Holland had been during the First World War. But in part it was due also to the instinct

of the government in power and its conservative supporters to observe a safe distance between themselves and the "threat" of the left,
especially in that period of depression with its alarming unemployment. It goes without saying that trouble with the powerful neighbors to the east was not desirable; anything that might stir up the
labor class at home should be avoided. It seemed best to remain
silent.

The history of the Second World War has some particularly ironic
lessons with respect to "the dangerous left." In the underground
press reports that here precede Ben Wessels' letters, one finds the remarkable topic of the "February Strike." This strike was a spontaneous event that had its center in Amsterdam in February 1941. It was
set off by repugnant anti-Jewish measures and actions. It was indeed
spontaneous, in the sense that very many took part in it without having to be coaxed. The appeal that triggered the strike, however,
came from the Dutch Communist Party, and though certainly the
strike was not a left-wing affair, the vast majority of the strikers
were precisely those who had suffered most under the crunch of
prewar unemployment.[9]

The prewar desire to maintain neutrality was a nonaction with as
yet invisible results, a nonaction that was very much related to the
mood of a government and a people who were afraid of change, any
change.

When change came, in the violent form of the German invasion
and occupation, the fear of change as a mental attitude was not
wiped out. And in truth, that fear, inherent in the middle class of all
Western industrialized nations, was never dealt a final blow. Especially in the last two years of the war, one finds endeavors in the illegal papers to outline what the nation ought to be like after the war.
The lines dividing parties began to be redrawn. *Trouw*, whose editors
and readers were rooted in a neo-Calvinist, politically conservative
circle, saw the need to liberate Indonesia (then still known as the
Netherlands East Indies) from Japan, to which end young Dutchmen
would have to prepare themselves to fight. *Het Parool*, moderately
leaning toward the left, gave lengthy thought to a new Dutch society
in which all parts would be truly and sensibly integrated; with respect

to the prewar colonies, the ideal of a commonwealth was stressed, the colonies freely choosing this integration with Holland. No one envisioned that the colonies would simply want out and break away.

Counting on change to come and anticipating the reality of violent change are not "natural" human abilities—similar to the lack of imagination in the sense I described above. The majority of people, in a village like Oostvoorne and everywhere, could not conceive of the fate awaiting the Jews. A most enormous topic for historical research and debate remains centered on the plans conceived to bring about that fate. Also enormous is the topic of the human lack of imagination for such fate at moments when ignorance could not be pleaded.[10]

A final word pertains to the variety of the selections that follow. The writers possess many different styles and many different ideological and religious convictions. These convictions are understandable to the reader but, at the same time, reveal certain uniquely Dutch circumstances.

As to style, readers will probably agree that on the whole *Het Parool* (parole, or password) is the best written of the papers. And without belittling the accomplishments of the others, it is fair to say that *Het Parool* shows a remarkable reflective ability. Many of the problems under discussion are considered from several sides. By contrast, *Trouw* (faithfulness) and *De Waarheid* seem to rush out foursquare and condemn the evil powers that have overtaken the land. Simplifying, one might say that the latter two spoke more clearly to a population in distress. They did this on the basis of what was central to each. *Trouw* identified itself to its readers at once as Protestant, certainly to the right politically, as well as religiously, and viewing the purpose of God and the House of Orange as two entities in immediate alignment. It paid great attention to each birthday in the royal family, far more than any other illegal paper. *Trouw* came into being as an offshoot from *Het Parool*. (To parliamentary historians, it is clear that *Trouw* represented a continuation of the prewar Anti-Revolutionary Party.) *De Waarheid* means *Pravda*, "truth," and never kept its communist stance and its sympathy for the Soviet Union a secret. The tone of its fierce, unwavering resistance to

Nazism is never far apart from *Trouw's* persistency, yet their views of what Holland would be like after the war certainly differed, and their ways would part when the war came to an end and formerly illegal papers suddenly became legitimate. One side, certainly not negligible, of the Dutch tradition is not strongly in evidence in the illegal press; it is the "liberal" group, in the European sense of being economically fairly conservative and not characterized by any religious commitment.

After the war, *De Waarheid* was for quite a while the most widely distributed paper in Holland. It had a most stirring career, but sadly it published its final issue in April 1990. Such postwar histories, however, would take us well beyond my present task. As far as the war period is concerned, let me add that even then the popularity of a paper was not always the right criterion for assessing its importance. And I most certainly cannot venture to say which of the illegal papers was most characteristically Dutch. Some papers had, in addition to their name, a special device on their masthead. Thus, *Het Parool* had the archaic-sounding words (taken from "Het Wilhelmus," the national anthem): *vrij onverveerd* (free and bold). Another publication, from which I do not quote but certainly did enjoy popularity, *Christofoor*, had "for God and Fatherland." By far the most popular device, however, came from *De Kleine Patriot* ("the little patriot," from which, too, I do not quote); it said: "Blijf optimist tot in je kist," a little ditty that means "Remain an optimist until in the coffin." Not a particularly elevated remark, but it did seem to embrace the nation most comprehensively, the cowardly and the courageous alike.

Notes

1. See the helpful work by Helen Fein, *Accounting for Genocide* (New York: Free Press, 1979), with an extensive bibliography (pp. 409–49). For much-debated historiographical problems concerning the Holocaust, see Michael R. Marrus, *The Holocaust in History* (Hanover: University Press of New England, 1987). The standard work on the fate of the Dutch Jews is J. Presser, *Ondergang: De vervolging en verdelging van het Nederlands Jodendom 1940–1945*, 2 vols. ('s Gravenhage: Staatsuitgeverij, 1965). The most elaborate description and documentation of events in the Netherlands during the

Second World War is L. de Jong, *Het Koninkrijk der Nederlanden in de Tweede Wereldoorlog,* 9 vols. ('s Gravenhage: Staatsuitgeverij 1969–79). In reference to Dutch Jewry alone, two documents stand out. Anne Frank's diary, written and concealed in the secret annex in which she and her family hid from the Germans, has become a part of world literature. No doubt, its appeal lies largely in the innocence of a child growing up, reaching toward a full human life, who will be dragged into a world of conflict and death. Anne Frank, *Het achterhuis, Dagboekbrieven 12 Juni 1942–1 Augustus 1944* (Amsterdam: Contact, 1947); translated by B. H. Mooyaart-Doubleday, *The Diary of a Young Girl* (New York: Modern Library, 1952). A new, critical edition, under the auspices of the Rijksinstituut voor Oorlogsdocumentatie, is *De dagboeken van Anne Frank* (Amsterdam: Bert Bakker, 1990), with the help of introductions and notes, insights into the legal aspects of the case, and new text care, by respectively Harry Paape, Gerrold van der Stroom, and David Barnouw; compiled by H. J. J. Hardy; David Barnouw, Gerrold van der Stroom. English translation by Arnold J. Pomerans and B. M. Mooyaart-Doubleday, *The Diary of Anne Frank: The Critical Edition,* prepared by the Netherlands State Institute for War Documentation (New York: Doubleday, 1989). The writings of Etty Hillesum, discovered and published more recently, made a great impression on the Dutch and soon thereafter also on many others, for within three years of the publication of her *Disrupted Life,* translations appeared in twelve other countries. Here we have a very different level of experiencing and witnessing. At the start of the war, Etty was already a young woman, and one who lived a conscious and passionate life with people and with art. Her writing gives us a perfect, literary image of those horrible days, and the fact that we see her choose to join the other victims of the modern world's destructive plan further heightens the drama of her books. Etty Hillesum, *Het verstoorde leven: Dagboek van Etty Hillesum, 1941–1943* (Haarlem: De Haan, 1981); translated by Arno Pomerans, *An Interrupted Life: The Diaries of Etty Hillesum, 1941–1943* (New York: Pantheon, 1984); *Het denkende hart van de barak: Brieven van Etty Hillesum* (Haarlem: De Haan, 1982); *In duizend zoete armen: Nieuwe dagboekaantekeningen van Etty Hillesum* (Haarlem: De Haan, 1984).

2. Jean Améry, *At the Mind's Limits: Contemplations by a Survivor on Auschwitz and Its Realities,* translated by Sidney Rosenfeld and Stella P. Rosenfeld (Bloomington: Indiana University Press, 1980), 48–50.

3. This information is given by C. D. Moulijn, *Opdat wij niet vergeten: Oostvoorne en omgeving tijdens de bezetting* (Brielle: privately printed, 1986), 21.

4. Moulijn, *Opdat,* 19, lists Pieter Langendoen and Mies Braal; they

offered hiding places. Pieter Langendoen and the family of Frans and Mies Braal keep recurring in recollections of assistance and resistance work in Oostvoorne throughout the war.

5. For Mauthausen, see Presser, *Ondergang,* esp. 1:93. The uncertainty with respect to Nan is a reflection of the needling uncertainty the Jews were subjected to from beginning to end under German measures. We should keep in mind that, in spite of the proverbial German sense for full documentation, *Gründlichkeit,* in all things, the plans for the destruction of the Jews were realized in many ways almost haphazardly. The following words by Abel J. Herzberg, concerning the impending fate of the Jews who were called up, rounded up, or temporarily left behind, are disconcertingly applicable: "If we may rely on the German documents, the Germans themselves were also in the dark" (Abel J. Herzberg, *Kroniek der Jodenvervolging 1940–1945,* 3d ed. [Amsterdam: Meulenhoff, 1978], 37–38).

6. As a result of postwar centralization, the population register is located in Rockanje-Westvoorne, where records are kept also for the village of Oostvoorne.

7. See the preface by A. H. Paape, the former director of the Rijksinstituut voor Oorlogsdocumentatie, in Lydia Winkel, *De ondergrondse pers, 1940–1945,* rev. ed. (Amsterdam: Veen Uitgevers, 1989), 7. This work was first published in 1954.

8. The increasing harassment and persecution of Jews is covered fully in the underground press. But in the course of 1944, there is a change. When the last Jews have been deported, the same papers become for the most part silent on the subject. The trite wisdom "out of sight, out of mind" may have its macabre relevance. (Without television, events that now shake *us* would almost cease to exist.) Many Jews, too, were "out of sight," in the sense that they were hiding. Targets of the German secret police, and not infrequently of collaborators among the Dutch police, they were "illegal persons."

9. The point is made by one of the most moving accounts of the Dutch resistance, H. M. van Randwijk's *In de schaduw van gisteren: Kroniek van het verzet 1940–1945* (Den Haag: Bert Bakker–Daamen, 1967).

10. One account, with specific reference to the "distant" country of the United States, is David S. Wyman, *The Abandonment of the Jews: America and the Holocaust, 1941–1945* (New York: Pantheon, 1985). (I need not underline that what concerns me is not merely a distance in space but the distance human beings create when they allow the curbing of their imagination in representing and feeling the suffering of others.)

Ben Wessels *(left)*, the writer of the letters, and Johan Schipper *(right)*, the recipient of most of them, 1941, the year before the correspondence begins. Courtesy of Johan Schipper.

Benjamin Leo Wessels. Courtesy of Johan Schipper.

Izaäk Wessels, Ben's father.
Courtesy of Johan Schipper.

Antje Wessels–van Dijk, Ben's mother.
Courtesy of Johan Schipper.

Nathan (Nan) Wessels, Ben's
older brother. Provided by Riet
de Leeuw van Weenen–van
der Hoek.

Carla Wessels, Ben's younger sister and the family's sole survivor, with nurse, 1956. Courtesy of Johan Schipper.

The Wessels' house in Oostvoorne (present, renovated state). Photo by Kees Bolle.

Ben's first postcard, October 13, 1942. Courtesy of Johan Schipper.

Plantage Franselaan. On the second floor, Ben and his family had their "happiest" time in Amsterdam. Courtesy of Leni Bolle.

A sampling of underground press publications. Courtesy
Rijksinstituut voor Oorlogsdocumentatie.

City Hospital of Amsterdam, formerly the "Jewish Invalid," the last residence of Ben Wessels in the city. The memorial plaque on the wall reads: "On March first, 1943, 24 Adari 5703, the residents of this building, formerly called De Joodsche Invalide, were taken away to their death. The iron of their chains became part of the building material of the state Israel." Photo by Kees Bolle.

Ben's high school diploma, signed by the director, G. Werkema,
December 24, 1941, when Jews were no longer allowed to attend
public schools. Courtesy of Johan Schipper.

Ben's letter of August 19, 1943 (*opposite*), in which he reports the arrest of
his parents. Courtesy of Johan Schipper.

Amsterdam, 17 Augustus '4:

Beste Johan en familie

Je zal het tragische bericht van de arrestatie
van Vader en moeder ook wel vernomen hebben.
Ja, jongen je weet niet hoe gelukkig jij op
het ogenblik nog wel bent al besef je het niet
Het ligt misschien voor jou wel af ik mij aan..
stel als een man van tachtig maar heus, ik
meen het. Hier is voor de rest niets bijzonders.
Alleen dat het bij ons in het gebouw een barende
drukte is De operatie patiënten van het
zieken huis waar Vader was zijn allen bij
ons. Ook de besmettelijke zieken. Voor
de rest zijn alle zieken doorgestuurd.
Je begrijpt dat het voor mij niet meevalt.
Als jongen van bijna 17 in een grote,
vreemde stad helemaal alleen te staan
valt niet mee. Maar laten we hopen dat
het nog voor korter duurt is. Kijken jullie
maar niet naar mijn schrift want ik heb
erge haast. Dadelijk moeten we weer aan
het werk. Schipper hartelijke bedankt
voor het roode leesdag hoor! Hoeveel had
het? Ook jij bedankt voor je kaarten
Johan. maar in ieder geval zijgen toeveel

het kost hoor. Je begrijpt zeker wel
dat ik me van de Clarinette afzie.
Ik zou geen lust meer hebben om zoiets in
mijn nabijheid te hebben te hard staan
te klespelen.
    Nu mensen, nu moet ik heus weer aan
mijn werk. Hartelijke groeten
        tot ziens Bert

A view within the camp of Westerbork. Rijksinstituut voor Oorlogs-documentatie.

The train ready to depart from Westerbork with a transport. Rijksinstituut voor Oorlogsdocumentatie.

Another view of the train. Rijksinstituut voor Oorlogsdocumentatie.

A drawing of the departure. Rijksinstituut voor Oorlogsdocumentatie.

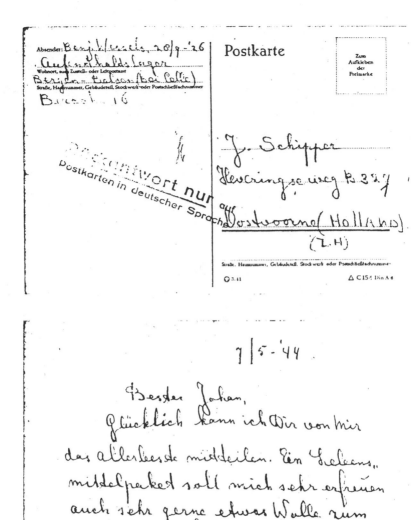

Ben's final postcard from Bergen-Belsen, May 7, 1944.
Courtesy of Johan Schipper.

Pit filled with bodies at the concentration camp of Bergen-Belsen, found when British forces reached the camp April 15, 1945. Rijksinstituut voor Oorlogsdocumentatie.

I W

INFORMATIE WERK

DER NEDERLANDSCH ISRAËLIETISCHE GEMEENTE TE UTRECHT

UTRECHT (Holland), 7-11-45
SPRINGWEG 164
TELEFOON 14742

Mevrouw J.W.Schipper
Oostvoorne Z.H.
Mevering D327

Geachte mevrouw Schipper,

Ref. W 449/452

In antwoord op Uw brief van 4 November delen
wij U mede dat ons omtrent
Nathan Benjamin Wessels
J. Wessels
A. Wessels-van Dijk
gegevens tot nu toe niet bereikt hebben.
Wij hebben de voorgenoemden personen in
de cartotheek van gezochte personen opgenomen
en zullen U berichten, zodra wij iets vernomen
hebben.

Omtrent Benjamin Leo Wessels moeten wij U tot
onze spijt berichten, dat deze op 22 Maart 45
te Bergen Belsen is overleden.

Hoogachtend,
I.W.
INFORMATIEWERK N.I.G.
UTRECHT

Dr.Landsberger

Official notice concerning Ben Wessels' death, dated November 7, 1945.
Courtesy of Johan Schipper.

Ben Wessels' Letters and Selections from the Dutch Underground Press

Bulletin. December 17, 1940

DUTCH SPIRITUAL FREEDOM
AND THE PERSECUTION OF JEWS

[. . .] The Netherlands probably have not gone through a month as dark as the one behind us since the infamous injustices of the Spanish domination. In our nation the Germans have begun their persecution of Jews.

Early in November we let ourselves be fooled. Obediently, we filled out the seemingly innocent little questionnaires, inquiring into our Jewish or non-Jewish descent. We would have done well to fear the spiritual dangers that threatened us with that questionnaire rather than the material risks we might have run if we had refused to a man to answer . . . The occupier would have been powerless, or at least disarmed for a while . . . As things now stand, by doing what we should not have done, we have enabled the enemy to bring down good Dutchmen. We must promise each other . . . never again to respond to questions that come to us from our foes and that are in conflict with our conscience . . . Let the German crime perpetrated in November be a lesson for us. Let us never forget how the Germans . . . dismissed officials, teachers, professors, judges, and many more, all native Dutchmen, solely because they were Jewish or of Jewish descent . . .

Each and every Dutchman has now lost his rights, has been handed over to false accusations and arbitrary loss of freedom. This is what the treatment of the Jews teaches us . . . One opportunity exists for us: the fact that the German mind is so ridiculously devoid of insight into human beings and approaches us in a way that is at the same time stupid and transparent. And yet, the danger of their propaganda remains. [. . .]

> [L. J. van Holk, professor of theology, Leiden.
> The author was, of course, unknown at the time.]

De Waarheid. December 1940

Lightning Rod: The Persecution of Jews

The German Nazi regime tries harder and harder to plant the poison of racial hatred in our land. The first official measures have been taken to discriminate against public servants and others who are "of Jewish blood." The Nazi regime paved the way for their dismissal and now intends to enforce it. Further attacks on the age-old freedom and tolerance of the Dutch nation can be expected, in view of the way the German Nazis carry on in the regions they have occupied and the countries they hold in subjugation.

In Belgium a "statute for Jews" was issued, whereby Belgians "of Jewish blood" or married to Jews are expelled from all public and authoritative functions and are given a special stamp in their identity card.

In Warsaw the medieval ghetto has been reintroduced. In Rumania, Bulgaria, and other dependent territories, anti-Semitism is rampant . . .

In our country, this Nazi production revolts us to such an extent that many . . . are inclined to regard this rage for persecuting Jews as some sort of barbarian madness. However, there is method to this madness.

The persecution of Jews was an important element . . . in preparing the war for loot that is now occurring. It was one of the means to instigate . . . the German people toward the conquest of new gains for the "Aryan" capital magnates. At present, the intensification of anti-Semitic incitement once again serves to make the German people swallow the continuation of the war for years to come and put up with the misery and the streams of blood that will result.

[. . .] We appreciate the gesture of the Netherlands Reformed Church, which addressed a request to the Nazi governor for retraction of the decree concerning the Jews, and which also made this request public. However, we cannot agree with the call for mercy included in that request. Resistance against anti-Semitic incitement is not a matter of mercy but of the national self-interest of the Dutch people. It is also a matter in defense of the freedom of faith, in the face of the wild threats the German press launched against the Netherlands Reformed Church because of the request.

The students in Leiden and Delft who decided in protest not to attend their classes provide an example for all of us . . .

The Dutch workers and all freedom-loving Dutchmen should fight this imported poison of hate against Jews as one of the means with which German imperialism wants to establish its system of slave labor here. [. . .] Dutch workers and all freedom-loving Dutchmen must fight this imported poison of anti-Semitism, through which German imperialism seeks to establish its system of slave labor here . . .

Het Parool. February 10, 1941

THIS WE DO NOT WANT!

The week of Sunday Feb. 2 to Sunday Feb. 9 has been a week of terror over the Netherlands . . .

It is difficult to remain calm. It is difficult merely to register what this week has brought us. Point by point, here is the list of German violations of justice [. . . — The paper goes on to list and discuss seven things, of which I reproduce four]:

1. Persons who practice a profession requiring an oath of office and who must be considered Jewish are permitted to practice their profession only for Jews after May 1, 1941. By means of this measure, our

Jewish physicians, lawyers, dentists, pharmacists, brokers, etc. are expelled from society in the Netherlands.

2. The Dutch identity card of whole or part Jews will be stamped B-I or B-II. "B" stands for "bastard." The low-life German brain could not have come up with anything more offensive and slanderous. Here the fruit of the spirit truly marks the venomous criminality of Nazism.

3. The Dutch book week has been prohibited. Reason: it does not show enough German books compared to the number of Dutch books. 75,000 copies of the "Gift book" [traditionally presented to book buyers at this annual event] will now be destroyed.

4. The festivity at actor Paul Huf's anniversary in Laren . . . was made impossible by members of the N.S.B. [Nationaal-Socialistische Beweging, the Dutch National Socialist Party], who were supported by uniformed Germans. Violent anti-Semitic demonstrations accompanied the events. At the same time, comparable degrading actions were unleashed elsewhere in the country, including The Hague. Everything happened with the . . . approval and encouragement of the German SS, the radical elements of the Nazi party, and the Green Police. The Wehrmacht, which has less of a liking for unrest and trouble in the occupied territory, yielded; it apparently is no longer able to prevail over the SS firebrands. In Amsterdam, shameful scenes occurred. In collaboration with the Green Police the N.S.B. tried to start a pogrom on the Rembrandt Square. [. . .]

[. . .] One cry rises up from all of us after this week of terror: THIS WE DO NOT WANT! . . .

WILL OUR CLERKS BETRAY US?

Last week, all practitioners of professions and offices who took an oath required by the state because of their profession or office received a circular, stating:

> In accordance with the order of the Rijkscommissaris for the occupied Netherlands territory, I notify you that persons who are required to take an oath . . . in order to assume their profession and

who have to be considered Jewish in accordance with article 4 of Ordinance No. 189/1940 of the Rijkscommissaris, have to terminate the practice of their profession as of May 1, 1941, but on the understanding that they are at liberty to remain operative exclusively for Jews.

In connection with the foregoing, a person who is to be considered Jewish in accordance with the above-mentioned article 4 is obliged to fill in the enclosed form. He/she must return the form to me, registered. Return should take place as soon as possible, within at most 8 days after the postmark of the present circular.

The Hague, February 5, 1941

[This circular came from the Dutch Department of the Interior; hence the title of the present article: "Will Our Clerks Betray Us?"]

[. . .] It is a well-known weakness in many sorts of criminals . . . that they want to be considered decent human beings.

The Germans too would like to keep up this pretense, and hence it is even more shameful that Dutch top officials, such as the secretaries-general, collaborate in this sad comedy and put their signature under such a measure. The Germans are now enabled to pretend this thing came about not at their order but on the basis of the will expressed by Dutch officials . . .

What are the Dutch lawyers, doctors, etc. going to do? Will they, who call themselves bearers of the *officium nobile* [noble office], follow suit and likewise haul down their colors for German injustice?

[. . .] The circular does not mention any sanction or penalty for refusing to return the enclosed form. As with all the crimes of the usurper, once more intimidation is expected to bring about the desired effect. [. . .]

The Horde in the Street

Encouraged by the German horde, the low-life rabble of the N.S.B. ventured into the streets again, intending to "win over" the public. Those who thought it best to ignore the action of the W.A. [Weerafdeling, the armed branch of the NSB] . . . learned during the past weekend that events begin to take on the shape of pogroms and that the violence in the streets is not limited to the mistreatment of Jews but is directed at everyone who has the temerity to appear . . .

The incidents that shook the capital on Saturday and Sunday occurred especially in and around the Kalverstraat [well-known shopping street] and the Rembrandt Square. The initiative was completely on the side of the so-called W.A. Sunday afternoon, armed N.S.B. gangsters attacked some cafés [. . .] that had not submitted to their terror, destroying the furniture and battering the guests. Jewish visitors were kicked out and chased into their homes. Many were pursued until they fled inside wherever they could, whereupon their persecutors smashed windows, forced their way in, flung pieces of furniture onto the pavement, grabbed radios and smashed them on the street. The events led to real battle scenes, because many of those attacked defended themselves bravely. Police and gendarmerie fought the W.A. bandits, so that afterward dozens of those Nazi heroes wound up in the hospitals of Amsterdam. During the clashes, the Green Police [. . .] appeared on the scene.

They ordered our police to stop the struggle, and the gendarmerie, who had so manfully arisen in defense, were disarmed in public.

The Hague too has again seen violence raging in its center. Protesting passersby and men and women wearing displeasing buttons were molested and assaulted.

In Zandvoort, the N.S.B. rabble, which had been ordered in from elsewhere, interrupted a stage play because there was a Jew among the actors! Incidents occurred also in Dordrecht and many other towns.

Prof. van Dam at Work

[Professor van Dam was secretary-general in the Ministry of Education.]

Some textbooks for instruction in French contained the following sentence in an exercise: "The French wines are better than the German wines." The other day the order came from The Hague that this sentence should be pasted over.

Prof. van Dam makes a stand in defense of the German cause and will no longer put up with such insults to the Reich — *l'imbécile!*

"Pressestelle" Prevents Disaster

The conception that the German is incapable of humor is decidedly incorrect. Only, his humor differs from ours; it is involuntary, and it is unconscious. Last week, the Pressestelle [the official German press bureau] in The Hague delighted the daily papers with news concerning a command from on high . . . that from now on no advertisements are acceptable concerning Eden hats, Churchill pipes, and Chamberlain umbrellas. This form of "English propaganda," the German censor decides, is "undesirable, and even intolerable."

Thus, thanks to the watchfulness of the Pressestelle, Perfidious Albion suffered another defeat, and a serious disaster for the Reich has been prevented. *Gratuliere, Herr Pressekommissar!*

Het Parool. February 17, 1941

The Anti-Semitic Bomb Burst the Wrong Way

[. . .] The battle in the Jewish quarter has become a splendid demonstration of national solidarity. Laborers, students, the unemployed, office clerks, and others went to the Waterloo Square to help their threatened Jewish countrymen, and when the anti-Semitic assassins came marching in military formation, intent on slaughter among the inhabitants of the poor Jewish quarter, they first bumped into a large troop of Jewish youths who had posted themselves before their dwellings for the defense of their parents. The horde of Kraut servants fell upon the Jews, who opposed them energetically and successfully. When the battle had barely started, auxiliary forces that had been kept at the ready poured forth from air-raid shelters, shacks, and porches to take their place beside their Jewish comrades.

The pogrom heroes were beaten back. In spite of the Green Police who fired repeatedly, the rabble of the W.A. received a firm punishment. Dozens of the bandits had to be transported to the hospital; since then, one has died.

What happened on this hazy, moonlit night can be considered a successful beginning of Dutch resistance against the Nazi banditry. Here, young men of the Netherlands, from various circles, the most diverse religious traditions, and all sorts of professions, stood shoulder to shoulder. [. . . What we witnessed] was the unity of the Dutch people that rose up in resistance to protect a menaced part of the people against the German and his servants.

The performance of Amsterdam authorities inserted one false note into this picture of national unity: police and gendarmerie were given orders to stay neutral. The police are not allowed to take action when a band of the N.S.B. attacks a decent Dutch citizen in the street, beats him up, perhaps kills him. There is no excuse for a mayor and a chief of police who issue such an order. Of course, the gentlemen have been under pressure and they act under German coercion. However, in such situations the task of Dutch authorities who understand their duty is to arouse a feeling of national honor in the masses. [. . .]

Pieter 't Hoen
[pseudonym of F. J. Goedhart]

O Heer aanzie!
Laagheid en onrecht hebben zich verbonden,
Een macht die al wat edel is vertreedt,
En elken dag ontwaakt men in het leed
En weet het leven in zijn kern geschonden.
Een leugen schalt langs wegen wijd en breed,
De waarheid stamelt uit vermoeide monden,
De laagste leuze heeft geloof gevonden.
Talloozen gaan in een bezoedeld kleed.
Het onrecht pocht: ik ben de nieuwe orde,

Mijn jeugd verstaat de wet van staal en steen.
De laagheid galmt: aan mij behoort het worden,
En mijn geweld vaagt eerst van eeuwen heen.
O Heer aanzie wat reeds in ons verdorde,
Want uit dit duister redt Uw woord alleen.
Marnix

[O Lord, regard!
Nobility and justice are no more.
Instead, the vile and lawless kill the good.
Each day bears woe more than we thought it could,
And life is damaged in its inner core.

Untruth resounds in town, in field, in wood,
Truth stammers, falters, finding voice no more,
While ears heed stupid slogans of the boor.
Too many of us are no longer good.

Injustice trumpets: "I am the new order;
My youth loves rules of steel and of concrete."
And vileness boasts: "I am the great creator;
My primal power is universal weal."
O Lord, regard what inside us has withered;
In this black night your word alone can heal.

The poem is archaic in form and expression, and "Marnix" is, of course, a pseudonym. Both, pseudonym and to some extent also the poetic form, are derived from the sixteenth- to seventeenth-century struggle of the Netherlands against Spain—a history familiar to the Dutch and unexpectedly inspiring anew. Marnix van St. Aldegonde (1540–98) was in all likelihood the poet of the Dutch national anthem.]

GERMAN TERRORISM IN THE CAPITAL

After the W.A. of Mussert [the leader of the NSB] had been chased out of the Amsterdam Jewish quarter and the black-shirted rabble no longer dared show itself in this neighborhood, for a moment anti-Semitic terrorism seemed to have ceased. However, this respite was not to last long. The German police took over the task of the W.A. terrorists. Since last Saturday afternoon, the Amsterdam Jewish quarter is in an almost permanent state of alarm. The Grüne Polizei makes the streets unsafe and makes innumerable arrests, at random, apparently with the intent of bringing the public into a state of panic.

Saturday afternoon the tumult began. Gray cars with Grüne Polizei moved in from all sides. Officers stood on the footboards, revolvers in their fists. The men sang anti-Semitic songs. Every bridge giving access to other parts of town was raised or occupied. They pushed into the Tip-Top Theater, where a stage play was going on. Spectators were violently chased outside. The young men among them were driven together with rifle butts. Passersby were beaten. In frenzied voices, the Germans shouted at everyone: "Bist du Jude?" [are you a Jew?], after which identity papers had to be shown . . . Very many were picked up and taken away. The number of arrests runs into the hundreds.

[. . .] For long hours, the same scenes were repeated on Sunday and Monday. The number of arrests is very large. Estimates vary from 400 to 1,000.

[. . .] In the meantime, under the leadership of Herr Böhmke, further measures are taken against our Jewish brethren. The *Herren* have conceived the idea of transforming the Jewish quarter into a ghetto. A recent count showed that, in a complex of streets that is known as typically Jewish and where some 13,000 people live, 6,000 non-Jews have their residence. It is obvious what enormous problems will arise when they try to execute their ghetto plan. However, for the German, nothing is too foolish. For him, acting out his anti-Semitic neurosis on the Dutch is an absolute must.

Apparently, the initial plan was to separate an area of streets from the city with a tall fence and to imprison the Jews behind it. This won't materialize, due to a lack of wood. Hence, a beginning has been made with barbed wire . . .

[. . .] Spontaneous protests occurred in various parts of the city. Today, Tuesday morning, employees of the tramways went on strike to protest the German barbarities. In the early morning, no tram was available anywhere. The public, though severely inconvenienced, gave their complete support to the striking conductors and drivers.

Just the same, the unambiguous protest of the tramway staff is not enough. There must be massive acts of protest. Not only the tram but also the railways should join the action, and likewise the power companies, and further, most especially, the shipyards, and other factories that work for the enemy.

Pieter 't Hoen

What Does the Enemy Have in Mind with the "Arbeidsdienst"?

Certain things make us extremely suspicious with respect to the "Dutch" Arbeidsdienst [obligatory labor service of young men in a pseudo-military, uniformed army], the newest institution the enemy has fixed us up with. This Arbeidsdienst is being organized after the German model. In Germany the *Arbeitsdienst* serves various purposes. It functions first of all as a place to hide the unemployed, so that one can boast that "es bei uns keine Arbeitslosigkeit gibt" [with us there is no unemployment]. The hapless ones who are hidden away in the Arbeidsdienst because of their unemployed state have to do heavy labor and receive in return a pitiful wage. Thus the Arbeidsdienst serves not only as a camouflage but also as exploitation of the unemployed. However, the institution has still other uses. It is also meant as an educational establishment for National Socialism. Therefore, in the long run, inevitably, the "Dutch" Arbeidsdienst will be under the direction of the N.S.B. . . .

LARGE STRIKES IN THE CAPITAL. POWERFUL PROTEST OF AMSTERDAM LABORERS AGAINST THE ASSAULT ON JEWS

[. . .] Tuesday, February 25, early in the morning, a strike broke out that soon assumed a general character. Streetcars did not run, and this sent a signal throughout the city for workers to put down their work. [. . .] In this way, Amsterdam's laborers expressed their opinion of the anti-Semitic persecutions . . . A livid indignation had taken hold of the city. Should we stand aside and watch as our Jewish brothers are mistreated? Should we pass it off with the classic question cowards have always raised on such occasions? "Am I my brother's keeper?" Yes, the people of Amsterdam answered, we shall make a stand for those who are burdened and oppressed, trampled and rejected.

The strike punched the German and his mercenaries in the nose.

Aghast, the German stood and watched. The strike confused him, and at first he did not know what was happening . . . It took him hours to regain his ability to act. But by then, the spontaneous movement had spread so wide as to be uncontrollable.

Zaandam turned out to have joined the capital, as did a number of businesses in Haarlem and some in Hilversum . . .

Everywhere, the strike was in the very first place a powerful protest against scandalous anti-Semitic terrorism a barbarous *Deutschtum* has unleashed upon our country. At the same time, however, the protest actions were directed against all the other injustices, the unfairness, the loss of liberty, . . . and the gradual starvation the German has brought over our land. Tuesday evening and the next day, manifestos were pasted over the posters the German had affixed everywhere. [. . .]

When the German finally understood what this massive protest amounted to, he at once began to take measures to stem the spread of the movement to more cities. Newspapers were ordered not to mention the events in any way. Radio transmitters were silent on the subject . . .

The manner in which the German attempted to stop the movement proves clearly that he has lost his head. The Grüne Polizei was sent into the streets in countless automobiles, and they began to shoot at everyone who did not make himself scarce. At some intersections, machine guns were set up to clear the streets. At many points in the city, hand grenades were used. The gray and green cars raged over the asphalt, machine guns rattled, hand grenades exploded, and in between came the sounds of German curses and the cannibalistic throat noises uniformed Nazis emit when they charge an unarmed and vulnerable crowd. Almost incomprehensibly, the number of dead has not exceeded ten.

Wednesday evening the Wehrmacht commander turned out to have assumed power in the province of North Holland. The announcement was published that in this area all political parties are banned, and wearing political uniforms and insignia is forbidden. This was a great success for the strikers. The Wehrmacht appears to have understood what caused and triggered the events. N.S.B. and W.A. were removed from the street, and the radical instigators of the NSDAP [the National-Sozialistische Deutsche Arbeiterpartei, or Nazi Party], the SS, and the Grüne Polizei—who were behind the scandalous anti-Semitic disturbances of recent days—were thus disavowed by the German commander.

Pieter 't Hoen

ROMAN CATHOLIC CHURCH MUST BE HIT

After an English bombing raid against an oil installation [in Rotterdam], the Germans followed with a punitive bombardment of the type that has become customary with them. In the first place it was to serve as a reprisal against a neighborhood [i.e., the neighborhood adjacent to the oil installation], from which somehow information useful to England had been sent out, and in the second place as an opportunity to lament enough civil victims over the radio and in the Nazi papers—an occasion the well-aiming English airmen do not often provide. We already know this Nazi method from Den Helder and Haarlem.

That night [fourteen days ago], the German heroes of the air decided to pinpoint St. Francis Hospital for punishment. While the bombers were prepared for takeoff, an Austrian made a telephone call from Waalhaven [airport of Rotterdam] to warn the hospital . . . As a result, most of the patients could be brought to safety . . . The director reported at City Hall that he had been warned and had taken his measures in time, 45 minutes before the hospital suffered some direct hits and five Catholic nurses were killed.

Razzias Against Jews

Wednesday, February 25, the notorious Grüne Polizei closed off the Apollolaan in Amsterdam, dragged a number of Jews living on this avenue out of their dwellings and carried them off for an unknown destination. Unsuspecting pedestrians who wanted to enter the Apollolaan were met with a roaring: "Bist du Jude?" Those who answered the question in the affirmative were referred to the police van. It was appalling.

Het Parool. April 9, 1941

Passion Week 1941

O Haupt voll Blut und Wunden,
Voll Schmerz und voller Hohn!
[O sacred head, sore wounded,
Defiled and put to scorn!]

Passion week in the year 1941. Passion music in churches and concert halls. Week of passion. Music of passion. *O Haupt voll Blut und Wunden* . . . And

Wer hat dein Augenlicht
So schändlich zugericht't?
[Who has done such evil
to Thine eyes' sight?]

Inevitably, we remember these verses from the St. Matthew Passion when we think of the burden weighing down the Dutch at the present time.

For a change, we won't speak of the terror in government or politics, the violation of our constitutional rights, Seyss-Inquart's breach of oath, but solely of the bodily harm done to people, the *Haupt voll Blut und Wunden* as it rises up before us when we think of the sadistic excesses toward the Dutch, and especially Jewish Dutchmen, of which the uniformed German hordes are guilty. That is the Passion story of the spring of 1941.

Man forgets quickly.

In 1933, the world turned away from the spectacle that was Germany: a public murder of the intellect, a bloody slaughterhouse where Jews and non-Jews were tormented and tortured to death. The reports were so incredible, it seemed so improbable that in this century a people and its leaders would descend to such barbaric and medieval extremes. Many shook their heads and said: "That cannot be true. That must be exaggerated!" [And so we forgot.] Yet reality was ten times more beastly . . .

We forgot.

Until the culture bearers came here from the east . . .

And thus the Netherlands got their own '33. We could see it with our own eyes. Now, that same

Haupt voll Blut und Wunden

Voll Schmerz und voller Hohn! rose up before us. And we ourselves asked the question, when we saw the victims beaten, when we heard the reports from the survivors . . . :

Wer hat dein Augenlicht

So schändlich zugericht't?

But even this terrible reality, here before our eyes, will fade if we do not make an effort to remember, if we do not continue to say to ourselves: "That is what they did. That is what they still do, every day. Therefore it is my duty to go on taking my share in the struggle for the liberation of my people."

Therefore we must not forget that they forced Jews to clean stinking toilets with their hands; that they forced little shopkeepers to sit hunched before their shops until they fell over, and were treated to rifle butts and nailed boots . . . that they made Jewish prisoners run around in rooms for hours, and tripped them with a foot, and that those who were clever enough to jump over the foot had their legs kicked from under them; that those who saw these things and betrayed their emotion or indignation by moving an eyelid or a corner of the mouth were beaten to a pulp; that many who were pushed to the extreme and rebelled had to pay for their despair and courage with their life.

Oh, we do not even speak of the degrading scenes in the Amsterdam City Theater, where men were packed together on the stage for not having been indoors in time during the notorious penal period imposed after the strike. Whoever opened his mouth to speak had to stand for hours with his hands up; Jews were beaten like dogs before all present; women who had first been made to scrub and mop the dirty waiting rooms of the Germans were forced to sit between the policemen in the hall, to listen to their filthy language, and to watch while they pummeled away on the stage and the Germans in the audience laughed and applauded each cruelty. The vocabulary of the culture bearers made the Amsterdammers blush with shame. For with civilized people this happens: they feel pain when they see human beings drag human dignity through the mud. Those who were in the City Theater at that time felt shame, because men acted like that to men . . .

Yet one comfort comes with this Passion Week: a cause that must be furthered this way, with the cudgel, the knife, the revolver, the bull's pizzle, the execution squad, is a lost cause.

Ik Zal Handhaven. July 1941

How to Act & How Not to Act

March 26, 1941. A German military man entered a building in Amersfoort during a concert and asked all Jews to leave. The entire audience left the hall.

A chief of police in Rotterdam made out an official report concerning his son's crossing to England. If the crossing fails, and his son returns, he owes the results to his father, a despicable Netherlander.

Het Parool. August 11, 1941

Jewish Obituary Notices

Obituary notices of Jews who have died in Buchenwald and other internment camps are permitted only in Jewish periodicals (the *Jewish Weekly*). In other words, the press of the Netherlands is not allowed to print them.

This is the latest supreme order of the German occupiers to the Dutch press. What difference does it make? Everyone knows that Jews who fall into Teutonic hands are exposed to the most terrible fate. No newspaper can suffocate this knowledge. On the contrary. The more the terrible truth is repressed, the starker it stands out.

Het Parool. August 23, 1941

The Requisitioning of Metals

The collection of metals for the benefit of the German war industry produced in Amsterdam about 80,000 kilograms of copper, lead, zinc, etc. Indubitably, this is considerably less than the Germans had imagined. At the same time, however, we have to establish the fact that it is considerably more than we might have expected on the basis of the anti-German disposition of the capital's population.

[. . .] A large part of these 80 tons comes from the living rooms of good and honest folks, whose only weakness was their cowardice; they could not refuse to respond to the enemy's summons. These spineless individuals do not yet understand that this total war requires the total stake of our powers. [. . .]

De Vijfde Colonne [Rotterdam]. August 1941

Buchenwald

[. . .] More than 60 years old, I was arrested as a reprisal for the treatment Germans in the Dutch East Indies had to undergo. Now, released again and back in the country, I want to let all of you know something about the way in which hostages are arrested and the treatment they have to undergo. Don't anticipate the bloody and sensational; it won't be part of my report. Besides, it would be superfluous. Read, and reflect on the reality . . . and you will understand that it is worse for our morale than anything else that has stained our history with blood.

In complete innocence, on the day of my arrest, I was picked up from my office and transported to The Hague. Only with great difficulty did I succeed in getting permission to say good-bye to my family and to collect some necessary toilet articles. All this took place under strict surveillance, and within half an hour.

Upon arrival in The Hague, I am given the reason for my arrest, and I meet my companions in misfortune . . . We are told to hand over all our possessions, including toilet requisites and underwear . . . and then we are put on transport. Our destination is Buchenwald, a name that is no more than a sound for us as yet.

We are taken by coach. After a full day, we stop, just beyond the border. Our lodging is an ordinary prison cell, where thirty of us have to spend the night, walking, standing, or lying down, but without a place meant for sitting or lying. The second travel day is like the first. But not the night. Again, our dwelling is a prison cell, again all thirty of us have to enter it, but now there is one bed. Exhausted, one of us falls down on it. Before an hour has passed, we have to undress and delouse him. The third day is spent again on a coach. Before we enter another place for the night, de Monchy [C. J. R. de Monchy former mayor of The Hague, now one of the hostages] lodges an energetic protest. It helps. Each of us gets a cell, and, at last, after three days and two nights, a pallet.

The fourth day, we reach Buchenwald. After an inspection we are told that we are honorary prisoners and will be kept separate from the others. Instead of our own clothes, we are given old, worn-out military garments.

Then an indefinite imprisonment begins! All days are the same, and we are not allowed to do anything. The only highlight is our weekly bath. We line up with bare upper bodies. Then into the cell. Quickly we take off the rest of our clothes, a hot shower, quickly put on the clothes, and then, chests bare, line up again outside in the cold, waiting for the others. Many among us died from pneumonia. Of course, you have seen names in the obituary notices.

The food is monotonous and bad, potato soup being the main course. The moral torture of a life without prospect or distraction is worse.

I get sick, and they take me to the infirmary . . . There, for the first time, I get to know something about the other prisoners, the Dutchmen punished for political reasons. From the ward I can see the inner court, and for a few days I witness the morning roll call. Every morning, the prisoners line up [. . .], their upper bodies bare. After a brief order, the Jewish prisoners step forward. A second order, and they all go and get a table from the inner court, and at once they line up again. A third order; they bow down over the table, and a whiplash shower comes down on the bare backs . . . A signal sounds, someone growls, the spades are shouldered, the march to the quarries begins. [. . .]

Het Parool. September 25, 1941

WE STAND BESIDE OUR JEWISH BRETHREN!

[. . . The list of scandalous measures against our Jewish compatriots is long.] The worst is the dragging off of young Jewish men to camps, where they die like rats. [. . .]

Only an undeveloped people like the Germans, suffering under political and cultural inferiority feelings, can become the matrix for a demented racial hatred . . .

Het Parool. November 15, 1941

OUR JEWISH FELLOW DUTCHMEN ARE ROBBED

Jewish Dutchmen continue to be robbed by the Germans.

Recently all antique shops that were in Jewish hands have been closed down and sealed. Supposedly this was to be done to save

"Germanic art" from "Jewish commerce." As it turned out, all art objects, antiquities, paintings, etc., that were found in the stores concerned were confiscated by the Germans. Moreover, the next step was to expropriate all paintings that happened to be in the hands of Jewish art dealers. Virtually all canvases seem to go to Germany, where they rapidly find buyers. Every German who is a bit endowed and who sees the collapse of the Third Reich in the offing pays fantastic amounts for paintings of little value. With this sort of investment they try to protect themselves against the inevitable catastrophe of the German Reichsmark.

Textile stores owned by our Jewish fellow citizens have also incited the German greed. Since November first, about 1,700 textile shops have been expropriated and shut down. The enemy has confiscated the stocks.

The German world reformer does not worry over the question of how the victims of such plunder should try to eke out a livelihood.

Het Parool. July 14, 1942

AGAINST THE DEPORTATION
OF DUTCH LABORERS AND JEWS!

[. . .] The Germans are engaged in committing their worst crime since the beginning of the occupation of our land.

[. . .] Tens of thousands of Dutch laborers and other productive workers are deported to work in Germany, in flagrant conflict with international law and the Geneva Convention.

And as a result of insufficient sabotage and resistance against this kind of deportation, we Dutchmen have now enabled the Nazi barbarians to make a beginning with their latest plan: the deportation of our Jewish fellow countrymen to work in concentration camps in Poland . . .

Het Parool. August 21, 1942

THE AGONY OF THE JEWS

The deportations of Jewish Dutchmen that started on a large scale in Amsterdam are now beginning everywhere. [The initial despondency and resignation that had overcome many among the Jews] has gradually given way to a spirit of resistance, even if this resistance is often marked by despair. Evidence of this includes the scanty response to the summonses. Each transport leaving from Amsterdam should consist of about 1,350 persons. These transports [by train] run by way of camp Westerbork in Drente, which serves as a sort of reservoir, and then on to Poland. At two of the last transports in early August, respectively, 120 and 350 persons showed up. On good grounds, the others preferred the difficult struggle for existence here to a sure perdition in Polish camps . . .

In the provinces the deportations go on unabated, and there too the turnout is often small. A good part of our nation has already realized that the no-shows must depend on the compassion of their fellow countrymen. Remain prepared to render such support and pay no attention to the threats of the persecutors. Soon the day will come when each one will be asked the question: "What did you do?"

De Waarheid. September 1942

NO END TO THE PERSECUTION OF JEWS

The roundup of our Jewish countrymen goes on and on throughout the land. In Amsterdam especially, this brutal manhunt is rife.

Lately, Jews who are summoned through the so-called Jewish Council to assemble at the train that would take them to the land of the dead have responded less and less to that summons. Every week transports of 1,300 persons are to take place, yet only hundreds or fewer appear in most cases.

This is possible only because of the massive help the general population has offered, providing temporary shelter and protection. Those who are most poorly housed themselves, the most destitute, are often the most generous in their hospitality and support. There are also instances in which some have abused the misery of the Jews by exploiting those who had a bit of money. This is scandalous.

The important point is that fewer and fewer victims show up to report when summoned. Nevertheless, the hunting season is open, and regularly we see city quarters cordoned off and homes ransacked, and people dragged away.

These days, [Paul Joseph] Goebbels informs us of another "secret plan." The Allies, upon their victory, would deprive German mothers of their children, according to him. It goes without saying that these are lies. The truth is that here in our land, before our eyes, the Krauts *are doing* precisely what they warn their followers about back home. It is the Dutch children who are torn from their mothers, only because they are Jewish.

[. . .] In Amsterdam, the roundup is no longer the work of the green Krauts [the Grüne Polizei], but of the so-called rifle brigade of the [Dutch] police. These are the brigands who sold themselves to the enemy and were trained in the camp of Schalkhaar, near Deventer. The camp leader, a certain Captain Donders, was recently arrested for black-marketeering: a typical sign of the sort of bandits these men are.

[. . .] This is the scum that now makes Amsterdam unsafe. At each of their operations, people assemble in protest, often to be dispersed by truncheons. These demonstrations must become more numerous and fiercer!

Kill these scum! Don't let them do their executioner's job for the enemy!

CAMP OF TORTURE: BUCHENWALD

Some items of information we received about the concentration camp of Buchenwald show us the frightening conditions there.

Prisoners get ten ounces of bread for an entire day, and a bit of watery soup. They have to labor in the quarries from early morning until late at night and are lashed on like animals. This is the camp where our comrade L. Seekers, city council member of Amsterdam, is imprisoned. Everyone who knew this comrade remembers his imposing figure. Before the war his weight was over 200 pounds. Now it is less than one hundred.

The prisoners are weakened to such an extent that when they catch a minor cold they often incur severe pneumonia. As a rule death follows within hours.

Some 60 men die each month in this camp. [Inmates] are tortured in the most sadistic ways. One wonders what the Krauts have in their minds when they slowly torture people to death. [. . .]

SAFETY RULES

In clandestine work, writing down names and addresses is forbidden. Only in extreme emergencies may one help one's memory a little by noting down signs or words.

Not a single outsider should be able to decipher these. It is proven, especially in case of arrest, that the very best thing is not to carry any notes at all except on matters of no significance whatsoever, which can at most lead the police astray . . .

Het Parool. September 25, 1942

CONTINUED DEPORTATION OF JEWS

All the crimes we have recorded concerning deportations of our Jewish countrymen pale when compared with the method applied in Amsterdam since the first week of September. Again, Jews are dragged from their homes, but now men and women 60 to 90 years old are singled out! Like the others, they disappear by way of Westerbork to "Eastland."

This seems to have become too much for the Amsterdam police. The task has now been assigned to the punks of the Dutch (?) "order police," . . . drilled in accordance with the Nazi system in Schalkhaar near Deventer. These butchers follow their prey like bloodhounds, and when they do not find the ones they came for at home, they pick up whoever happens to be there.

Amsterdam, Oct. 13, 1942

Dear Johan and family,

Let me sit down and write another card.[1] I am happy to say we are fine. If you people knew what the Jewish Council did for all of us you wouldn't believe it. We have now been moved to a new address. Our old address was Adama van Scheltemaplein 1. We were there at the Center for Jewish Emigration. Now we are, I'll write it down clearly, B. L. Wessels, Jewish Council for Amsterdam, Jan van Eyckstraat 15 Expositur. Now that I am writing this down it occurs to me that you better not write just yet, for I don't know how long I'll stay. Right now we get 8 pieces of bread with coffee, so you see how it is. I am curious what has become of our house. But I'm sure I'll hear about that.

That was quite a night we had in Oostvoorne. Father and I will surely never forget it. If we had known that here things were going to be as good as they are we certainly would not have worried so much. Johan, show this letter to Ina[2] and everyone we know. Writing a lot costs money, and we have each of us only 7½ guilders. Well Johan, I am going to stop now with greetings also for Pietje and Kruina[3] and the family.

Ben

B. L. Wessels, Joodse Raad,
Jan van Eyckstraat 15 Expositur

1. The collection as preserved begins with this postcard.
2. Ina Pleit is a girl who is often mentioned in the letters. She was close to the Wessels family, especially to Ben's older brother, Nan.
3. Pietje and Kruina Schipper are Johan's younger half-sisters.

B. L. Wessels
p/a A. van Os
Plantage Franselaan 34
Amsterdam

Amsterdam, October 15, 1942

Dear Johan and family,

   Finally, I can write a longer letter. How are you people doing?
We are fine, and even more beautiful, we have been released from
the Center Tuesday afternoon. Now we are with relatives. It was
quite a relief to be in the open air again. Anyway, that's behind us,
and we'll hope that it won't happen again. I guess you mustn't mind
the pencil writing. My fountain pen was taken away. My entire
equipment with backpacks and six woolen blankets is gone. But that
doesn't matter. The most important thing is to get out of it yourself
safe and sound. How are things at school? Do you still have to get
there by tram? And how is our house! Anyway, you'll have to let us
know about things soon. I long for a letter. I am getting a job here
with the Jewish Council. Then I'll have something to do again. I
couldn't believe what was happening when in the evening I could
once again do something as common as sleep in a bed and sit on a
chair. But all that I'll tell you in person some day. That pocket flashlight, the one with the generator, they also took from me, there opposite the bandstand in Oostvoorne. We were frisked completely,
and whatever they could use, money, in fact everything, they took
from us.[1] That day Mother had already been picked up in the afternoon. That night was frightful. But I'll tell you all about it myself
sometime. For the moment you shouldn't tell anyone that I am free,
except Ina and Jaap,[2] well, you use your judgment. But for the rest,
nobody. The family van Dijk,[3] we were with them, they are going on
to Poland. Well, I've written a bit again, and I am looking forward to
a letter soon. With greetings also from Father and Mother. Ben.
   How are Pietje and Kruina doing?

   1. Before leaving Oostvoorne, Ben and his father had already been robbed
and maltreated by the German Ortskommandant (local commander) and his

men. The Ortskommandant was a Wehrmacht officer, hence must have acted on his own initiative. Fear must have prevented Ben Wessels from referring to him here in writing. See also the letter of July 30, 1943.

2. Jaap Tieman, a young man of Nan Wessels' age, was a neighbor on the street where the Wessels had lived.

3. The van Dijk family was the only other Jewish family in Oostvoorne. Antje Wessels, Ben's mother, was Mr. van Dijk's sister.

"ROCKET FLASH" AMSTERDAM CABARET SOCIETY OF THE POST, TELEGRAPH AND TELEPHONE SERVICE

Secretary: Miss R. R. Os — Amsterdam — Pl. Franschelaan 34 upstairs[1]

NO. Amsterdam, Oct. 20, 1942

Dear Johan and family,

I'll take a moment to write a note. This morning I received your letter. How are you? With us everything is still the same. At the present I am employed with the relay service of the Jewish Council, which means that as a sort of messenger I have to do errands all day long throughout the city. It keeps me very busy. Doing nothing. What's new with the evacuation ideas in the village? If it goes that far and you have to leave, please don't forget to send me your address, for otherwise I can't reach you anymore. How is everything else in Oostvoorne? It will be best for all sorts of reasons not to talk with everybody about me. My backpack, my blanket bag, my shoes, everything I had in my backpack is gone. All of it went with the transport to Westerbork. Fortunately, here everything is quite peaceful. I have barely left Oostvoorne, but it seems like two years. Johan, if you can get hold of a flat battery, I would be enormously happy. Here in the city nothing is available. The family van Dijk has been sent on to Poland. Very bad. How are Pietje and Kruina? Luckily, I was able to take my musical instrument to Mr. van der Hor in time.[2] How is the family Kamman[3] doing? Give them our regards. Jaap and

Ina too. Now you have heard from me again, and I hope for a quick answer from you. Best regards to all five of you from all of us, especially from me.

Ben

P.S. Best regards to "Grandma and Grandpa Schipper." If you can get more batteries, please do. We also need the round type batteries.

Ben

B. L. Wessels
p/a Mr. A. van Os
Plantage Franselaan 34

1. The stationery mentions the name Os in the letterhead. The family Os (or van Os), with whom the Wessels were now lodged, are the relatives mentioned in the preceding letter.

2. Ben played clarinet in the local wind orchestra. Mr. van der Hor was its conductor, and the instrument was the band's property.

3. The Kammans were a retired couple and next-door neighbors of the Wessels.

Amsterdam, Oct. 31, 1942

Dear Johan, family,

First, I have to thank you, as does Mother, for the letter I received. We were very happy with it. I should thank you for the batteries, also on behalf of my cousin. I kept one of them for myself. I had just thrown a letter into the mailbox a few minutes before yours arrived. What else has happened with all of you? We are all right, fortunately. I like my (new) job very much. It's hard work, but that doesn't matter. I have to work on Sunday, but then, I am off on Saturday. Probably Sunday will be free again next week. Do you have a lot of catching up to do? Do you have to work during the vacation? How come you have a vacation anyway? Now you are saying under your breath, what a nosy devil—but I feel pulled, just like iron to a magnet. I imagine that Mr. Werkema[1] will feel mightily pleased that

all of you are sending packages to him. In the house with us here is
another boy, evacuated from Zierikzee. I like his company. He is just
as old as you. Almost every night we sit and play checkers or chess.
I suppose you visit Ina a lot. It's a pity for you that it isn't summer
now. You could go into the High Bush[2] and sit on a bench with her.
You needn't blush, your mother has known about it for a long time.
I guess I had better stop talking about this, or else they won't let you
go there anymore. Well, I am coming to an end again, with best
regards, and see you!

Ben

1. Mr. Werkema was one of the teachers and director of the high school
Johan and Ben attended in Hellevoetsluis. Together with his fellow teacher
Mr. Schoenmaker, he was among the hostages taken by the Sicherheits-
polizei and placed in the camp of St. Michielsgestel, near s'Hertogenbosch.
2. High Bush, het Overbos, a wooded area in the village.

[A letter from Ben's mother is added:]

Dear Johan & family,

I very much want to add my greetings. We were very happy with
Johan's letter. Fortunately we are healthy, and we were pleased to
hear from all of you. We'll hope for the best for the future. With
kind regards also for Ina, Jaap & all friends and acquaintances. As
ever, your

A. Wessels v. Dijk

Also kindest regards from my husband.

De Waarheid. End of October–
beginning of November 1942

Use All Your Power to Stop Further Deportations of Jews!

The horrifying mass deportations of Jews are going on uninterruptedly. Supposedly only 20,000 Jews are "permitted" to stay in the Netherlands, and this for the sole purpose of making the continuation of anti-Jewish cruelties possible also in Holland! In big cities, the newly trained Schalkhaar bandits are employed for the *razzias* on Jews. It is a shame upon the nation that Dutchmen will do such things . . . In the provinces too, Jews are tracked in their hiding places. There, N.S.B. constabulary do this foul work. The fate of the deported Jews is horrendous. [. . .]

Following a brief stay in a camp . . . they are sent on toward the east, and families are torn asunder. Not only are fathers separated from wives and children, but also the mothers must leave their little ones behind. The transport itself is beastly. Pushed into luggage vans, standing, the victims endure a journey of days. Whatever little they could bring with them is not permitted to go on the transport. In Assen [in the province of Drente], cargo halls are filled with suitcases that Jews had to leave behind. It is terrifying, and the Dutch people put up with it! True, there is some splendid solidarity proven to Jews who hid before the Nazi executioners. But that is not enough!

Protest, Dutchmen, you who have always lived in friendship with the Jews! [. . .] Act massively against the *razzias!* See to it that here and there a Schalkhaar bandit disappears! Explode in acts of protest as you have shown yourselves capable of in the February days of 1941.

[. . .] Here again it is true that the sacrifices of the struggle are many times smaller than the losses you suffer in acquiescence!

De Waarheid. November 1942

ABOUT THE UNDERGROUND SECOND FRONT

[. . .] In the south of the Netherlands a train with victual derailed. Locomotive, cars, and cargo were a total loss.

In the west, large stores of the Wehrmacht went up in flames. Damage was considerable. [. . .]

The English air force has launched attacks on trains and railway yards. In Heerenveen a train was taken under fire. The locomotive was heavily damaged. In Hoogeveen a railway yard was bombed . . . At Steenwijk a train was taken under fire. The locomotive broke down; cars loaded with straw burst into flames . . . In all these instances a considerable number of railway men were killed and wounded. These are the consequences railway men must accept as long as they go on doing their work for the Krauts. May there soon be an upsurge of resistance among them! Let them make a beginning by refusing to drive trains with Jews in transport!

Amsterdam, November 8, 1942

Dear Johan and family,

Here are just a few words, in the hope that everyone is healthy, which can also be reported about us, fortunately. Things are going well enough in their way. Getting up early, and working hard during the day, but life here suits me very well. What are you up to on your vacation? I guess you spend half your time in the grape hothouse or playing with the new cat. Johan, you can perhaps convey our regards to Nel Lobs[1] on the Molenweg. Kruina and Pietje, you have my thanks for the picture postcards!

I'll get around to sending a beautiful one to you in return. I loved them. Have you managed to learn the ["]Tannhäuser["] yet?[2] Every Tuesday and Thursday I go and listen to a concert. It takes place here in the institute. It's really worthwhile. Today was a day off, and with my friend I went across the Ei on the ferry to Amsterdam North. Johan, if you have a picture of yourself, send me one, will you? I don't have any anymore. The weather here is bad most of the time. Rain and nothing but rain. I have to be at my job in the morning at a quarter past seven, then we first eat, and finally, a quarter to eight we start work. We used to begin at eight, but now it's three quarters earlier. How is Ina? Is she still at the rationing office? Would you be able to get a pair of wooden shoes for me, size 42? What about asking Mr. Holleman whether some pair isn't there in the house? We were very surprised to hear about that. We did not know about it. Anyway, that is not so bad.[3] Do say hello to Jaap Tieman when you have a chance, and ask him what about those five guilders? Well, after all this I am through placing orders, except for the best wishes also for Grandpa and Grandma Schipper from all of us, especially from me.

Piet

Piet Zeldenrust[4]
Jan Laagwaterstraat 342
Amsterdam C.

1. Nel Lobs, a girl, was an acquaintance of the Wessels family, especially of Nan.

2. The wind orchestra, in which Johan played the flute, and in which Ben had been playing the clarinet, was rehearsing the overture to the opera *Tannhäuser.*

3. The family Holleman was living near the airfield in the coastal area used by the German troops and had to move. The surprise Ben mentions was apparently caused by the news that this family had been quartered temporarily in the Wessels' house. (Later, German officers moved in.)

4. This is the first time Ben uses a pseudonym—probably more out of youthful playfulness than for real protection.

Amsterdam, November 11, 1942

Dear Johan,

I'll take this moment to write just a postcard. How have you been since this morning? I feel sure you're all right. As to me, I am in even more excellent shape than before. Fortunately, I found my mother again, and also the family van Dijk.[1] Of course I cannot write everything that happened. Now I'll quit again. All the best for the rest of the family and Ina from your friend

Ben

1. I have no information about what had happened to Ben's mother. The joy of finding the family van Dijk again—presumably they had been sent to Poland (see letter of Oct. 15, 1942)—is understandable.

Amsterdam, November 17, 1942

Dear Johan and family,

Finally, I have another chance to write. How are things in Oostvoorne? I read your letter and took in the news. That's the way it is. You people will have to suffer through the same thing we had to go through, even though it won't be by far as bad.[1] It is also very bad for your Grandma and Grandpa. Anyhow, it is the same for all those people. There have not been any changes for me. Father still has nothing to do, and Mother is busy every day in the household, together with my aunt. Johan, if you want to, you could do me a terrific favor and send me a pair of long laces, if you still have those out there. You can't get them here anymore, not anywhere in the city. I'm afraid that you won't be attending the Ulo because of the evacuation. Our beautiful village is taking tragic turns. Before I forget — you should give our regards to all our acquaintances. As for the address, you must not give it out, really, *absolutely* not!!! You should give my greetings especially to Wil Rijnders. You can always do that by way of Ina. But besides that, you can do it personally. I feel quite content in my job, and fortunately I can adapt well to this place. But don't think I won't come back when things get to that point. Believe me, I'll be back twice as fast as I left. And for sure, that means very fast! Do you still do anything about saving stamps? Here I don't do anything about it anymore. Whenever and by whatever chance you people have any leftovers, anything will be gratefully received. Here we have only a meager production. Not like Oostvoorne. The band is also likely to meet its end before long, if things go on the way they are going. Please, write at once when you know more. We have still not received any signs of life from Nan. Since August 24, that is a long time. If only some message reached us. Today, during my work, I went and listened to an operetta orchestra. Bert van Dongen was among the musicians. Every Tuesday and Thursday afternoon they come out here in our building. All right, family, I have let you know a little again, and I hope to hear some news about Oostvoorne from you soon. Best regards and wishes for a speedy "get together," your friend

B. Pietersen[2]
Laag Waterstraat 59 upstairs
Amsterdam

1. The news Johan had conveyed concerned the German plans (and especially people's apprehensions about these plans) for evacuating many villagers.
2. Pseudonym, as in the letter of Nov. 8, 1942.

[A letter from Ben's father is enclosed:]

Amsterdam, November 17, 1942

Dear Johan & family Schipper,

First our special greetings, and I can report of our health what we certainly hope also about all of you.

Possibly Johan would do Ben a favor. Ben wants to give a [rationing] coupon to a good acquaintance here in Amsterdam, but they no longer accept it here.

Possibly Johan would not mind trying to exchange it in Oostvoorne. Ben has no time, and already started work early. Possibly I too will be able to get a job in the Jewish hospital and I shall of course accept it immediately.

Your letter has been received in good order and it is always a special occasion for us to hear something from Oostvoorne. For although we are in Amsterdam we are nevertheless real Oostvoorners and continue to live in our feeling with you and all the people in Oostvoorne.

Regards for all our good acquaintances. Also for Ina, Jaap, Kamman, v. Es,[1] and for all who inquire about us.

More next time.

Greetings especially for all of you from

the three of us

Iz. Wessels
Read the greetings from Pietje and Kruina and liked them

in haste

1. Like the Kammans, the van Es family were also neighbors in Oostvoorne.

De Waarheid. November 21, 1942

The Jewish Camp Westerbork: An Accusation

In [the Dutch province of] Drente, many kilometers from the inhabited world, on a soggy heath plain where one sees church towers only rarely on the horizon, is the gate of hell.

From the plain a chimney rises. It is the chimney of the kitchen of the Jewish internment camp, Westerbork. Before the large Jewish camp, a small camp stands; this is where the bloodhounds are trained, the "tough Teutons" of Dutch extraction who are here to acquire their "heroism." Guns slung over their backs, they stand guard around Westerbork . . . Supervision inside the camp is provided by the Dutch constabulary. Some among them disapprove of the measures taken against the Jews, but they "serve" and do their "duty," . . . and actually assist in driving Jews into the transport trains destined for Poland and elsewhere. Such trains consist of the oldest and dirtiest German railroad carriages, and sometimes also a few cargo vans. They are packed with men, women, and children, sick, healthy, old and young . . .; some of the carriages in between are for the Nazi butchers. The transports are pulled by Dutch locomotives with Dutch engineers and a Dutch chief conductor. Whenever next morning a transport is to leave, those who are destined to be on it are named during the night and must pack their things. And again, it is the Dutch constabulary who are the agents in this act.

In the camp, men live in barracks, separated from their wives and children. There is a roll call for the men each morning at 7:00 . . . After the roll call they march off to work. Among other things, they are building a railway to the camp that will facilitate the transports. From a distance, those who are thus employed can see the loading of the transports . . . Often they are themselves taken away with a transport.

Around this pool of misery, adjacent to the barbed wire, and in full view of the camp, stands a row of wooden villas. These are the dwellings of the gentlemen officers of the SS. . . . These SS officers are also Dutch—at least by birth.

The Jewish internment camp is an accusation against the Dutch nation for allowing things to go so far.

[. . .] Not only has a duty toward our Jewish fellow citizens been ignored, *but in addition, . . . the Dutch have paved the way for the mistreatment of all Dutchmen.*

Westerbork is an accusation, but also a warning! Expand your action against the persecutors of Jews! Do not limit it to hiding Jews who have fled. Protest in all possible ways against the anti-Jewish measures! Railway men, refuse to drive transport trains! Patriots among the constabulary, refuse such services to the Nazis! Dutchmen, obstruct the police street by street in their act of dragging Jews from their homes . . . May Westerbork call forth the struggle that we postponed too long.

Amsterdam, December 6, 1942

At last I have another chance to write. How are all of you? We are still all right, fortunately. We'll have to keep in mind that each day is one more in the count. Father has gotten a hospital job, like me. Before I forget, it will be best if you write back to me in the same manner. Alas, we still haven't heard anything from Nan. That is very bad. You people cannot imagine what such a thing means. Last week a couple of letters came in; and then, when they pass by your door again, it is terrifying. All right, this you will understand. Carla[1] is doing very well. We still get a little letter from her every two weeks. She is in better shape than any of us. Why don't you give regards to Jaap and Ina. I did not give the address. I know all about it. (?!) Kruina, I read in the newspaper that you did your very best at the Gymnastics Club show. Is that true? Does my instrument have a player again? or is it still lying around? From time to time I still think of that morning in the tram, when we did not know where we were going. It seems as if that was years ago. It's a miracle that I saw you then. But that's another thing we'll come to talk about. Everything passes so fast. Now winter is upon us again. I don't think it's likely I'll be with you on New Year's Eve. Johan, thanks a lot for the laces. I needed them very much. I'll really make up for all of it! I suppose you get home much earlier now that you go by bicycle again. I wish I could say something like that about myself. I read that you too will qualify for running around with a bit of green next year.[2] You'll love it. I myself would find it quite an honor, but they don't talk to me about those things. All right, I have been writing to you again about this and that, and I hope to hear from you soon in return. Kindest regards and the best wishes from the three of us.

[Not signed]

1. Ben's younger sister, who was seriously retarded, was probably in an institution in Amersfoort at this time.

2. "Bit of green" is an oblique reference to the uniform of the Arbeidsdienst, the German-imposed labor service.

Dear Johan and family,

A moment for a short letter. How are all of you? We are well,
luckily. Life is quite monotonous. Leaving at eight in the morning
and home at five. It's exactly the same as it is with you. You probably
have to leave at eight for school. I also go to a course here in bookkeeping, commercial arithmetic, business theory, language, and
style. It's really something. But now that I have a chance to do these
things here, I may as well go ahead. You never know, it might come
in handy. It's true that it is not easy for me, but that doesn't matter.
The course is Sunday mornings, half past nine and goes on till half
past one. But now some talk about something else. You'll have your
birthday on the 31st and I have already bought a present for you that
will certainly come in handy. Your father can take advantage of it
too, for he'll surely like it as much as you. I had been thinking about
a zoology book, but I couldn't get hold of any. It isn't necessary
these days to decide what you want. You may be thinking: he is far
too early for my birthday. But things are like this: it's a terrible time
for us here, and we don't have the vaguest idea today whether we'll
still be here tomorrow, and just imagine that we won't be here anymore, and then you, Johan, will at least have had your birthday
present. Of course, you should not take it in the sense that we'll no
longer be here next week, for that's not how it is, but there is a
chance. I crossed half the city for that book. I went to a meeting
here where they played magnificent music. Violin and piano. It
would really have been something for you. You can't imagine how I
long to speak with all of you once more, and to walk around again
near you people. But things are the way they are. Plodding along
and worrying. That proverb, East, West, Home's best, we really feel
that now. For the coming Christmas I wish you pleasant days. The
best thing is to enjoy those days at home as cheerfully as possible.
That's always much better than to just let them pass. Anyway,
friends, I'm coming to an end now, and I cannot but wish you a
happy new year and peace soon, and of course a reunion before
long. Do convey the very best regards to all our friends. Would you

believe, I almost forgot to congratulate you, but my congratulations are heartfelt, really. Ben

You will notice that the short letter I started out to write has turned into almost two letters.

[Added note from Ben's mother:]

Dear Johan and family Schipper,

I am happy to add a few words to Ben's letter. How are all of you, and Pietje and Kruina? All right, we hope. We are healthy and really at home here with our relatives. For the rest, we'll just wait and see. We only hope that soon we can return to Oostvoorne, near our friends and acquaintances. Still no report from Nan, and that is very sad for us, for we crave a letter from him. There are letters coming in here from Poland, but they do not speak to us. Johan, I congratulate you on your coming birthday and wish you a pleasant day, and I congratulate also your father, mother, Pietje and Kruina.[1] Wishing you also a pleasant Christmas and a happy new year, and following that, peace in the very near future. Good-bye dear folks, many greetings, until we meet again.

Antje Wessels v. Dijk

1. According to Dutch custom, not only the person who celebrates his or her birthday but all relatives are congratulated.

[Added note from Ben's father, in part scribbled between the last lines of Ben's letter:]

Dear Friends,

I am happy to add my good wishes to those of my wife and Ben, and I congratulate all of you, and Johan in particular. Enjoyable days, and a happy New Year in peace.

Cordial greetings, your friend I. Wessels

That the Jews Be Extinguished

How often have the German Nazis deceived their victims? The Krauts use the cowardly . . . ploy of putting their prey at ease in order to kill them more easily.

[. . .] That is how it has been with the deportations of Jews. The cruel Krauts went out of their way to reassure their victims; thus they could be shipped without protest to the destroyed eastern regions. Supposedly the purpose of all this was to put the Jews to work, just like other Dutch laborers in Germany. Of course not under equally "favorable" conditions; but for the rest, they would be treated decently and would be assisted by their own people of the Jewish Council. It is understandable that some of those tortured victims, cruelly torn from their homes, talked themselves into believing that things would not be too bad in the Jewish camps of Poland.

In their wild, medieval rage, Hitler and his gang have sworn to exterminate the Jews. The Jews are the butt of their revenge for failure to win the war. This crime is executed systematically and in cold blood. A new proof is the decree of the SS butcher Himmler, that before the end of 1942 all Jews in Poland must be exterminated. The decree has been disclosed by the Polish government in London and by the Jewish Agency in Palestine. Alas, it must be deemed authentic. In the next four weeks, hundreds of thousands of men and women, boys and girls, the young and the old will lose their lives. It seems unthinkable, and yet, it is true. Once in Poland, a sure death awaits the unfortunate . . .

Amsterdam Terrorized

When the Nazis suffer defeats on any front, you can be sure that terrorization of the occupied territories increases. The worse the defeat, the more insolent become those noble Teutons . . . against defenseless civilians. They know well that the allied successes reverberate in the occupied lands and ignite the spirit of resistance. Fearing this result, they seek to avert it with their acts of terror.

Friday, November 27, Amsterdam has witnessed another wave of arrests. Each time, one thinks it cannot get worse, but the monsters always outdo themselves. The greens and the blacks [the armed, black-uniformed Dutch collaborators] swept across Amsterdam and emptied factories where Jewish girls were working. They picked up the non-Jewish girls as well . . . Police vans and trucks took away the victims. Streetcars were used too. They were commandeered, the public forced out, and the girls were forced in . . . Jews were arrested in the street. Store clerks were also picked up in the same sweep. Not only young people, but also the old and the invalids, all were driven into the Hollandse Schouwburg [the theater serving as the point of assembly. . . .]

[In this same Dec. 12, 1942, issue of *De Waarheid*, the article on Westerbork, published Nov. 21, 1942, is reprinted.]

Het Parool. December 23, 1942

PERSECUTION OF JEWS NO END IN SIGHT

The sadists of blood and soil, with their insane racism, do not tire of thinking up tortures and terrors for the Jews. In the weeks behind us, in Amsterdam alone, another 9,000 Jews have been picked up and dragged away. It seems the Germans want to reach certain "successes" before Christmas in order to celebrate their "Weihnachten" in sentimental bigotry around the Christmas tree, striking up hymns about "Peace on Earth" and so forth. The carolers will be the very ones who in the last few weeks arrested the Jewish employees of stores and workshops, deprived the others of their identity cards (which means deportation to Germany), and stole the machinery from those workshops . . .

De Waarheid. January 2, 1943

THE PERSECUTION OF JEWS MUST BE STOPPED

In recent weeks, a powerful campaign against Hitler's inhuman persecution of Jews has been waged in the Allied nations. The governments of Great Britain, the United States, and the Soviet Union have published a joint declaration in which those responsible for this mass murder are threatened with the most severe penalties. [. . .]

In the meantime, the Krauts go about their beastly business. Reports that arrive from the occupied Soviet regions make our blood run cold. Now that Hitler's hordes are beaten back by the Red Army, they vent their rage on the defenseless who remain in their clutches. The bloodbath of Lutzk, on which radio Moscow reported, will be inscribed in history forever. Of the 19,000 Soviet citizens driven together in the Lutzk ghetto, 18,000 were murdered this past week.

These events were triggered by a German order that all males, including the smallest children, had to be castrated. The entire ghetto refused to submit to this atrocious order, and the Jewish physicians charged with the execution of this crime were steadfastly refusing as well. Thereupon trucks appeared in front of the ghetto; for days on end they carried off the inhabitants. At the execution site they parked in long rows until it was the turn of their passengers to die. The victims were taken from the trucks, and each group had to dig one deep pit to serve as their grave; then they were mowed down by machine gun . . .

Amsterdam, January 4, 1943

Dear Johan and family,

How are all of you doing after 14 days? We are all right, fortunately. I have said this before, so perhaps I am repeating myself, but that is better than not saying it at all: I wish all of you a better year than the past one was, and let's hope that what we had to say bye-bye to for a while will come back soon. And also I wish you, Johan, and of course the entire family, many more years at the occasion of your birthday, and we'll say: next year better than this. Then we hope to be present again, with our whole family. With us everything is running as usual. Only, we have to make do, plod along, because we have no "things" anymore. It is so hard to get anything. What have I heard? Did Werkema and Schoenmaker[1] come back? If that is so, do give him[2] my greetings. How do you like the book? Do you find it useful? You had better take it as it is. As far as books are concerned, you can't get anything anymore. Just remember, if it's not much, the intention is good. If in earlier days I had known how much work I would have to do, I would have conked out. Now I don't know better anymore. Soon we'll get a report card in that bookkeeping course. It is buzzing outside constantly.[3] Yesterday also. Actually, almost every evening. I have learned my way around here pretty well by now. Yesterday my friend and I went through half the city. Amsterdam is very beautiful. You really should come out here and see for yourself. That would also be nice. What has happened to the tram? Never mind, I do not need to ask. I know it as well as you do. How are Pietje and Kruina? Further, I suppose that everything in Oostvoorne is still the same. You should really think of coming out here and telling us all about it yourself. All right, dear people, I'll finish again with the best greetings, and let's say in our Dutch way: *tot kijk* [until we see each other].

Ben

P.S. In which hospital has K. B.[4] been admitted?

1. One of the teachers in the Hellevoetsluis high school. See also the letter of Oct. 31, 1942.
2. In all likelihood, Ben thought of Werkema, a teacher he admired.
3. A reference to the sound of the RAF planes flying over the city.
4. "K. B." — Kees Bolle — I was hospitalized for a while in Haarlem, near Amsterdam.

De Waarheid. January 1943

A Boxing Match
Holland–Germany

A match between Dutch and German boxers was staged in the Concertgebouw of Amsterdam. The well-known Dutch boxer Luc. van Dam took part.

For three bouts the Dutch were victorious, and the match became an antifascist demonstration; the public showed its sentiments so vigorously that the guests of honor, Deputy Chief of Police Bakker, Mayor Voûte, and the military commander-in-chief, General der Flieger Christiansen, soon had to leave the hall.

When the German Muller appeared in the ring and gave the fascist salute . . . the public filled the hall with a concert of hisses and boos.

[. . .] But in the final match the tumult reached a climax. From all sides came the shout, "Beat the Kraut to a pulp!" [. . .]

World Protest Against the Persecution of Jews

Since the blood decree of Himmler, calling for the extinction of all Jews in Poland by the end of 1942, a cry of horror has resounded through the civilized world. Never has a power anywhere had the gall to demand such an abject, cold-blooded mass murder of millions, for the sheer fact that they belonged to another race . . .

[. . . British Minister of Foreign Affairs Anthony] Eden has declared: ALL PERSONS WHO HAVE ISSUED ORDERS FOR THE MURDER OF JEWS, HAVE EXECUTED SUCH ORDERS, OR HAVE COLLABORATED IN DOING SO, WILL BE PUNISHED BY DEATH AFTER THE WAR.

In other words, punishment will be meted out not only to the SS bandits in Poland and Germany, and not only to the Nazi leaders and followers, but also to ALL who carry out their orders. Our "good" Dutch policemen and constabulary, who for months have hunted down Jews and transported these countrymen of ours to Westerbork, who there keep watch over them, and who take them to Germany, incur guilt of a capital crime and will be punished by death.

There is still time to refuse, and avoid the guilt of this crime . . . Whoever goes on with their executioner's work will have to bear the consequences, and the verdict will soon be carried out. [. . .]

De Waarheid. January 18, 1943

[. . .] If there had been a second front in west or south Europe, Soviet troops would long since have begun the decisive offensive . . .

Amsterdam, January 23, 1943

Dear Johan and family,

How are you folks doing? With us everything is still all right. You did not get the letters because of a misunderstanding, but before you start worrying, I'll write right now. How are things in Oostvoorne? I would love to come and look around for a bit. I feel such nostalgia. But we'll have to be patient for a little while longer. Only a very little while, because I don't have much time left. I do hope that things won't take very long any more. Anyhow, running matches are now held everywhere.[1] I have already been posted on a high place,[2] but I never spotted anything coming. At this moment the time is half past nine in the evening. Exactly at the point when I wrote down the word "matches," the doorbell rang. You can probably tell by my handwriting. We got terribly frightened, but fortunately there was a happy ending. If this were summertime, you would think there were mosquitoes, because of the zooming[3] sound in the aire (maybe I haven't spell[ed] this the right way, but it doesn't matter). Will you tell Mr. K. that I did not receive a canteen. It would be a terrible pity if that had gotten lost. How are Pietje and Kruina — well, I would actually like to list all the names in Oostvoorne. How marvelous those vacations always were at your home. I surely hope to come and stay with you people again this summer. Do you still have many guests? Or do they have to leave? How are things with Uncle Toon?[4] I always liked him very much. A new tailor shop has opened in the village, right? Does H. v. d. B. still attend the H.B.S., or did he decide to look for something still higher than that?[5] Okay, okay, now I'll stop the questions. I've got to ask one more, though: would you be able to buy a pair of wooden shoes for me, for I need them badly for my work. Well, Johan, I am coming to an end, with the best greetings, also from Father and Mother and my cousins, your family friend

Ben

1. A reference to *razzias*.
2. As a lookout.
3. Another reference to airplanes.
4. "Uncle Toon" was Toon Langendoen, one of the many who were evacuated from the coastal area. He was lodged with a family near the village center. He was married to a sister of "grandma Schipper." The endearment *uncle* shows the Wessels' intimate relation to Oostvoorne.
5. "H. v. d. B." refers to an acquaintance of high school age. "H.B.S." refers to the Rijks Hogere Burgerschool in Brielle, a high school of a higher grade than the one Johan and Ben attended in Hellevoetsluis.

Amsterdam, February 2, 1943

Dear Johan and family,

I suddenly realize that I did not write to you yet. The mailman will be here any time to collect this letter. How is life with you and our other friends? With us everything is still in order. We have another terrible day behind us. Constantly, day and night, the chosen people are pursued. Today they were in the "Jewish Invalid," where I am working. Nothing less than the Grüne.[1] They always take the aged and those who were granted a respite because of sickness. Now I really don't know anymore whether I wrote to you this week or not. In any event, if I did, I have forgotten. Tonight we have again been studying hard, both my friend and myself. It is so very difficult, and yet it's no more than a "flea bite" for me. We still haven't heard anything from Nan. February 14 he'll be gone half a year. Letters from Poland do come in occasionally. They are all very optimistic.

The way things are, if we have to go there, things can only turn out better. Worse is hardly possible anymore. Would I be with you again this summer? This is the way we talk all day long. But I do believe we can say "Yes!" We just have to be patient a while longer. Three weeks ago they came and took away my aunt and uncle,[2] in whose house we are living, but fortunately they are still in Westerbork. You know that's the place where Nan was at first.

Well, people, I am finishing with the best greetings, from Father and Mother, especially from your friend Ben.

P.S. I have gotten some watchmaker's tools, and I am going to repair alarm clocks again.

1. Grüne Polizei.
2. The family van Os in the Plantage Franselaan.

Amsterdam, February 15, 1943

Dear Johan and family,

It is ages since I've heard from you, but I understand the reason quite well. How are all of you? Fortunately, all of us are still together, though things have become especially difficult. Despair is growing. It's very bad here. People are being picked up all the time. They have come also to us more often and picked up someone who was here in the house. Also the hospital where I work is on the list for a clear-out. Yes, Johan! Living here is no fun. I have heard crazy rumors about you people. If they are true, there isn't a stone left standing. For what I hear is that the whole village was shot to rubble. Is there any truth to that rumor? Wednesday of last week, I went to the English course for the first time. For the sake of distraction, I've decided to add it to what I am doing. I spend all my leisure time studying. That's the most useful way to spend it. You had better not pay attention to my handwriting, for I have to write very fast.

We still have not heard from Nan. He's been gone now since August 14. How are Ina and Jaap and the others? Why don't you answer with a long letter. Receiving and writing letters is the most beautiful thing for us. I would really like to ask how old you are now. We have been arguing about that here. I say you turned 18. Mother said you were a year younger. Who is right? I would also like to have a small picture of you. I lost the photo of the two of us. That happened that morning, you remember, when we met in the tram. Are things at school still as usual? I just can't imagine that with all of you everything's running normally, while for us everything has changed completely. Well, people, I am finishing again with the very best wishes from Father and Mother and especially from me

　your family friend

　(formerly)?? Ben

Trouw. February 18, 1943

THE GROUND OF OUR RESISTANCE

Can we be content with the response of our nation in this time? Resistance is on the increase, they say. It is possible, even probable that this is the case. Certainly, the Germans do not leave a stone unturned to inspire it. [All of the German actions in Holland] can only evoke rage and hatred, and hence a feeling for resistance in our nation . . .

Admittedly, resistance exists, or rather, there is a spirit of resistance.

But is it the right spirit of resistance? Is it good enough? In these matters, we should be demanding.

[. . .] Opposition against the tenth penny [the 10 percent tax the Spaniards imposed on the Netherlands in the sixteenth century] triggered a great revolt. The purse of the people had been touched . . . Thus [King] Philip [II] and [his governor, the third duque de] Alva fanned the resistance and weakened the position of Spain. But the Dutch people were not born from resistance against the tenth penny. The nation arose from a resistance for reasons of principle. It was born from the will to preserve freedom of faith and conscience, so that God could be served in accordance with His Word.

Something like that is relevant now. The measures the Germans are taking are in a sense like the tenth penny. That is why the spirit of resistance we observe does not prove much on behalf of our nation.

After all, it is no virtue to be enraged about having to go to Germany and endure all the disagreeable things that that entails. Neither is it a virtue if for that reason one goes into hiding.

It is no virtue for an individual to resist being fleeced.

It is but natural that we wince at the sight of our people being mistreated and our culture being trampled on.

The spirit of resistance resulting from all this is no resistance of fundamental significance; it does not guarantee the inner strength of a nation.

[. . .] The foundation of resistance must be our loyalty to our government and country. Such loyalty is a legal obligation; yet it is not a formality. And neither is loyalty to Queen and Fatherland something romantic. The real meaning of our government and our country is: the historical state of the Netherlands, the historical Dutch nation, a state and a nation with its genesis rooted in spiritual struggle, and for that very reason a state with a spiritual calling.

What the Germans want, and what the Germans want from us, runs counter to that calling. This obliges us to resist. We are to defend a civilization that came into being under the spirit of the gospel . . .

What the Germans want, and what the Germans want to lay upon us is heathendom. The antithesis. And that is why only resistance remains for us, only resistance on principle, total resistance. It is not possible, and not permissible, to swallow a little bit of heathendom, for tactical reasons . . .

[. . .] This war is a spiritual war. In essence it is a war of religion. It is a struggle in which faithful Christians, Protestants and Roman Catholics, must fight side by side . . .

[. . .] This is the struggle of the Christian Church, which does not return to the catacombs but stands in the field of battle until she conquers definitively . . .

WATCH OUT FOR THE CENSOR

The Germans exercise more and more censorship of mail. So more than ever, the rule for all is:

Think before you write,

And, writing, think again.

Het Parool. March 5, 1943

THE WORD OF THE CHURCHES

[The text of a letter sent jointly by the Protestant and Roman Catholic churches in the Netherlands to Seyss-Inquart, Rijkscommissaris, the chief authority appointed over the Netherlands:]

The Protestant Churches and the Roman Catholic Churches in the Netherlands feel compelled once more to address themselves in full earnest to you, Mr. Rijkscommissaris.

They have turned to you several times before to take exception to the continuing injustice to the people of the Netherlands. The churches feel profoundly affected. They have raised their voice in accordance with their calling in Christ when in public life the principles anchored in the gospel are attacked. They point in particular to those principles that make up the foundation of our people's Christian life: justice, compassion, and the freedom of convictions and philosophy of life. They feel it their duty to witness that the authorities too are subject to the Divine law and must abstain from acts that are condemned by that law. The churches would stand convicted if they failed to point out to the authorities the sins committed by them in their exercise of power, and refrained from warning them of God's judgment.

The churches have already spoken of:

the increased state of lawlessness;

the persecution unto death of Jewish fellow citizens;

the forced inculcation of a view of life that is diametrically opposed to the gospel of Jesus Christ;

the obligatory Arbeidsdienst as a National Socialist educational institution;

interference with the freedom of the Christian school system;

enforced labor of Dutch workers in Germany;

the execution of hostages;

the arrest of many and their lasting imprisonment, including church office holders, in such circumstances as to have led to the death of a terrifying number of people in concentration camps.

At the present time, a new offense has been added to this list; it is the hunt of thousands of young people, their seizure and abduction.

In all these acts God's righteousness has been violated. The churches witness against vengefulness in our people and raise their voice against hate and revenge. In accord with God's Word, no one is allowed to judge on his own. But to the same extent, the churches are called to preach this word: "We should obey God rather than men." This word is a guide in all conflicts of conscience. It is a guide for those who are called up under the present circumstances. For the sake of God's justice no one may cooperate in acts of injustice, for that makes one an accomplice to the injustice.

Mr. Rijkscommissaris, in obedience to their Lord the churches address this word to you; they pray to God that He may lead you to restore the justice that has been so damaged in the exercise of power.

Trouw. March 12, 1943

Facts you should know:

— All town halls are guarded from five o'clock in the evening until eight o'clock in the morning.

— Railway stations in Haarlem, Amsterdam, and Utrecht have now and then been cordoned off and the public present frisked. [. . .]

— Most recently, old and sick Jewish citizens who had been left home until now on the basis of medical attestations have been taken away.

— The entire Jewish Invalid [the name of the hospital that was Ben's final abode in Amsterdam] has been emptied . . .

Amsterdam, March 15, 1943

Dear Johan and family,

Let me make use of the moment and write a few words. How are all of you doing? We have heard what happened in the village. What misery the war brings about! I am back to work. At the present time, I am employed with . . . the Grüne Polizei. Isn't it funny, and yet it is true. I had to go work there. Maybe I have a chance this way that I won't have to leave. What a funny world. Just imagine me sitting there at work with my star on my chest. It really isn't bad, so I can't complain. I am elevator operator for the moment. But all in all, I would rather be with you folks. I assume you yourself haven't received any notice yet, have you? We still haven't had any sign from Nan. Is Ina still living there? Give her, and also Jaap, my greetings. At present the situation is hopeless for us. Wouldn't you feel like coming over and visiting us some Saturday? That is the only day off for me. There is no danger involved at all, really! I suppose you do know that the family v. D. has been here, don't you? You will understand that we are dying for the sight of familiar faces. I heard that Bl. is also gone, and that de K. is living there now. Is school still in session? My course is still going on, but I myself cannot attend. Sunday is no longer a day off for me, and that is when the course was held. Now I have to try catching up at night. English has come to an end again. The man who taught it is also gone. I am shocked to notice that it has become terribly late and time for bed, so I'll end again with the best wishes also from Father, Mother and Carla,[1] and especially a firm handshake from your friend

Ben

1. Apparently, Carla had joined the family. This event was not stated anywhere in the letters.

Dear Johan and family,

How are all of you? With us everything is still going as we hoped
it would. For the last 14 days nothing much has happened to us.
There's nothing doing around here that's new. At the moment I am
elevator operator in the building where I used to be before. But now
in a different way! The night before last we were up and about all
night. There was a big fire diagonally across from us. You may have
read about it in the paper. Today, my boss told three of us to transport a load of crates with a pushcart. Just when we came to an inter-
section with lots of traffic, all the cargo tumbled onto the street.
That was a lot of fun for a change. This past night did not give us
much rest either. There was so much traffic (in the air) that one had
not much of a chance of sleeping. How did the Volharding[1] performance come off? I suppose a lot of people showed up. One thing is
certain: as long as I am not part of it, I am not going to be content. I
am getting bored stiff. I would not mind living here in normal times,
but now there's nothing attractive about the place. No, I would prefer Oostvoorne any time. A while ago Father saw a couple of Oostvoorners here. One really longs for acquaintances. As far as my
work is concerned, I am not in bad shape. I now have a nickname.
All personnel, a couple of hundred people, have taken to calling me
Koenraad. You know, of course, the fellow from the picture in the
newspaper.[2] Carla is going to school again. She is making great
progress. She even walks to school by herself, through the city. She
has really grown up. Well, we all have our work here. Say, Johan, do
write next time how things are with Ina and Kobi[3] and Jaap. All of us
are so eager to hear about them. By all means, give them our greetings. And how is Piet Langendoen[4] doing? I already knew before you
wrote about it. It's terrible that it had to take this turn. That's how
things are: each day can be too late for many. We haven't heard anything from Nan yet. However, some sign of life did come in of a few
people from Goeree en Overflakkee who left together with Nan. But
that sign did not come by mail. I notice that I have been writing

quite a bit, and hence, it's about time to finish, with warm regards for all of you, also from Father and Mother, especially from me,

Ben

1. Name of the wind orchestra.

2. Koenraad was the name of the ideal Germanic boy on posters for the Arbeidsdienst.

3. Kobi, or Kobie, was one of Johan's classmates and sister of Ina Pleit.

4. Pieter Langendoen was one of the most active and courageous underground workers in the village. (See C. D. Moulijn, *Opdat wij niet vergeten: Oostvoorne en omgeving tijdens de bezetting* [let us not forget: Oostvoorne and environs during the occupation; Brielle: privately printed, 1986], 35–40.) What the "terrible . . . turn" Ben mentions in the following sentence refers to is no longer possible to establish in the multitude of events.

Het Parool. April 5, 1943

The Gestapo released thirty Jews from Westerbork and provided them with railway passes. Their mission is to track down illegal activities; if they are successful, they will be rewarded with their freedom.

We issue an urgent plea to our readers: Be silent. Don't be misled by a star or sentimental talk . . .

Amsterdam, April 13, 1943

Dear Johan and family,

First, a very friendly yet urgent (!!!) request to you, Johan! This is the request: Will you come here as soon as possible, because I am in urgent need of you. I read your last letter in which you write about the difficulties of the journey. I do understand that it would be very difficult for you to arrange it. That's what I would have thought. But inquire with some acquaintance, for instance Mrs. v. D. in the forest, or the neighbors, family K., or someone else like them. You know what people I have in mind. But don't postpone it. You can always show this letter to one of them, if it has to come to that. Your father and mother would be very good also, that goes without saying. How are you all? I almost forget to ask. Here with us things are a bit gloomy, as you have been able to read in the newspaper recently. We ourselves are all right, but for the rest there is much to be desired. At least as far as the situation goes. I am still employed, although I do find myself in a rather hot spot right now, but maybe it means more of a chance to stay here. Although I don't have any illusions about that anymore, either. And moreover, if I stay here and my father and mother and Carla have to go away, that wouldn't be a barrel of fun either. Right now I am once more an elevator operator in the building of the gentlemen. I was archivist for a while. But I'll tell you all about it presently in person, for surely, I count on it that you will come soon. No matter how, do write on what day and at what time you'll get here. Last night I also wrote a letter to you, Johan, but that one must be burned later for "tactical" reasons.

All right, people, I am going to end again with warm regards also from Father and Mother and Carla, and especially from your friend

Ben

P.S. If I were you I would write only what date and what time you are coming. Nothing else.

I've enclosed a stamp for your collection. I bought this one at a kiosk.

Trouw. April 30, 1943

After Three Years of War

When this issue reaches its readers, the date on which we became involved in the war will be very close, perhaps already past.

We have suffered three years of tyranny, and oppression by the enemy still increases.

[. . .] No matter how much we have lacked in our efforts at resistance, no matter how weak we have been at times in our conduct, one thing is certain: we are still alive.

The enemy has not brought us down.

[. . .] He lures, and then threatens, then he shoots, but he does not win, not even when many of us stoop now and again.

He enjoys no credit with our people, he has none of their sympathy. [. . .]

The utter completion of misery holds a promise.

It means that the end is in sight. The measure is almost full.

The darkest hour has come before the dawn.

Why should we deny it? Occasionally we came close to losing heart in the three frightful years behind us. Sometimes we were surrounded by darkness. We had hope and faith. It was hope against hope. But it was real faith, the evidence of things not seen.

Now we feel that we have not hoped and believed in vain. We see points of light. Soon comes the shattering of the yoke.

The Netherlands will be restored. [. . .]

About Our Physicians

The resistance of physicians against the *artsenkamer* [an institution of the occupation requiring membership of every practicing physician] . . . has had its next installment.

First, our doctors had renounced their accreditation, as by doing so, they also lost all relationship to the *artsenkamer* . . .

The Germans were angered by this removal of the word "physician" from the name plates of our doctors. Of course, it smacked of a collective demonstration against the *artsenkamer*.

Through Deputy Secretary-General Verwey, the Germans let it be known that they considered the renunciation a fake, as indeed the doctors disavowed their qualification yet continued to practice medicine. The Germans declared they would regard the doctors' gesture as directed against themselves, and demanded that the name plates be restored to their original form.

For their part, the doctors did not object to this. Their quarrel was not with their own name plates but with the *artsenkamer*. [. . .] They sent the following letter to the secretary-general:

To the Deputy Secretary-General of the
Department of Social Affairs
Scheepvaarthuis
Amsterdam

In answer to your letter . . . , I am bringing the following to your
attention . . .

The information I addressed to the President of the *artsenkamer*
had no other purpose than to exempt myself from membership in
the *artsenkamer.*

The only way to do this was, according to the regulation itself, the
divestment of medical qualification with the resulting forfeit of the
right to bear the title of physician.

However, I do not at all intend to endanger public health. I am
continuing my medical activities because on the basis of the law on
the exercise of medical practice of 1865 I most definitely consider
myself entitled to do so. Nevertheless, I want to point out once
more that I do not consider myself a member of the *artsenkamer.*

If the occupying force is of the opinion that I am not entitled to
practice medicine as a result of maintaining my statement, I am still
prepared to accept this consequence.

(there follows the signature of [each] doctor)

It is obvious that our physicians have held to their resistance in
principle against the National Socialist *artsenkamer* in spite of the
threats against them. The people of the Netherlands should clearly
see the meaning of this struggle. What is at stake is not some private
interest of doctors who happened to be harmed by the Germans in
the way they harm so many private interests.

What is at stake is the interest of the Dutch people itself. Will
health care be guided in a National Socialist or a Christian way?

Will the goal be the cultivation of a strong race, and the eradica-
tion of the weak? Or will public health be served as it has been until
now, whereby all those in need could turn to their physicians with
confidence?

[. . .] The doctors have stood up for Christian morality against the
pagan morals of National Socialism. [. . .]

OUR MAYOR

The mayor of my town is quite a fellow!

He has always been faithful, always good for the town. He looks after each inhabitant. He is watchful of the interests of the citizenry as a whole. He does not behave like a despot, he does not act haughtily, he has the right word for the occasion, he does not brag, he speaks to all who want to speak with him.

He is like a father to the townspeople.

They are delighted with him.

I am fond of him myself.

That's why I am so sorry that now I must hold a few things against him. Had he not done these things, I could live more peacefully.

When the enemy demanded measures against the Jews and lists of names of which the purpose was to repress especially those people, who were just as Dutch as I myself, he did their bidding.

When the . . . town council was done away with and the unchristian Führer concept introduced as the guiding principle for city government, he was amenable, and since then he has been the Führer of our town . . .

When the names of our beloved queen and of Her children were to be removed from the street signs of our town, he did so without protest.

[. . .] When the enemy wanted to steal my bicycle for the sake of his warfare against my country, my mayor called on the entire magistracy and the police force to do it.

When I refused to go and work in Germany for the enemy against my own country, he, being chief of police, bore with it that his servants put me under arrest and handed me over to the enemy.

When my son refused to enter the Arbeidsdienst and be educated according to National Socialist principles, he, being so ordered, dragged my son from my home.

[. . .] Honestly, I believe he does not intend harm. He still does a lot of good. Who knows how much that was directed against me and my fellow citizens he has prevented? He is still the same amiable, popular man. He helps when he can.

I don't understand it. What has happened to the one great thing: to serve the queen . . . ? And how can he serve the enemy?

[. . .] My mayor is quite a fellow—but he should not be my mayor anymore . . .

Het Parool. May 10, 1943

A View of the Hell in the Concentration Camps

[. . .] A year and a day ago, the National Socialist riffraff swore by all the saints in the calendar that stories about ill-treatment in the concentration camps were "gruesome propaganda."

The total unmasking has come. We have before us the unmistakably true reports of a group of Dutch judges. With the consent of Dr. Wimmer, the commissary-general of legal affairs, they visited camp "Erica"—what a lovely name—near Ommen; they spoke with prisoners, and they saw the guards "at work." [. . .]

Prisoners Speak Out

Not for nothing do the Germans threaten to kill any prisoner who upon his release might tell about the camp . . . Some of the prisoners [interviewed] were prisoners in camp Ommen, some in camp Heerte, near Wolfenbüttel in Brunswijk. In the latter camp, daily rations for the 800 prisoners consisted of half a pound of bread and two pints of a watery soup. The least offense was punished by withholding that food. Whoever was sick, because he did no work, was given less than the normal portion. Hygiene was pathetic. The toilets, which were few in number, were stained with bloody, and of course extremely contagious, diarrhea. There was no doctor. The "sanitation man" who functioned as nurse had no knowledge of nursing and was virtually inactive. The custody of this camp is entrusted to "Dutchmen!" Their doings are impossible to justify. They beat a prisoner with a rifle butt, breaking his jaw, because he tried to pick up a piece of bread from the mud. Hunger tormented the prisoners so horribly that they did anything to get out of the camp. They tried to mutilate themselves by letting vehicles drive over their arms or pinch off fingers. Some also tried to be shot dead by the guards by refusing to work. Oftentimes the condemned in Heerte fell down dead, finished off by hunger . . . The corpses were placed in coffins to the jeers of the guards. Was the deceased too tall for the casket? The guards broke his legs in half . . .

From Heerte to Ommen

Nourishment was better in Ommen than in Heerte, at least in the beginning. In our estimation, it was even better than it used to be in Vught, where conditions that cried to heaven improved somewhat only in the last few weeks. (This has no bearing on the students in Vught; they are well off.) By contrast, the maltreatment in Ommen verges on the incredible. Some of the condemned in Ommen have been knouted unconscious on the ground. Many a convict has died under this treatment. The "bunker" punishment is also used . . . Here a prisoner is confined in a subterranean hole too low to stand up in. A narrow pipe brings in some air from outside, but no light. Inside, the floor is covered with water. No chair, no bed, no "john." One can only imagine. In such holes Dutch prisoners have had to spend up to fourteen days and nights . . . Gradually, it became customary in Ommen to punish each infringement of the rules, even the lightest, by withholding the food ration. Consequently, the prisoners succumb to malnutrition. In a few months' time, 169 patients were brought into the hospitals around Ommen, and medical statements appended to the judges' report prove once and for all that the camp of Ommen intends to expose people to death by starvation. "The majority of prisoners reach the hospitals in a condition of complete exhaustion, so that the least medical complication can mean death." [. . .] Of course, when the Krauts can no longer keep up their lies and denials, they take a different route: ever since the juridical investigation, transport of prisoners to the hospitals has been stopped. Now the poor wretches die in the camp, tortured to death by the guardsmen of Mussert, traitor-in-chief of the Dutch people. They die—because they have done something that in German eyes is "not permitted," or because a thoughtless judge condemned them for an ordinary crime to detention, which must be served not in a prison but, thanks to the

Germanic order, in a camp such as Ommen. Praise God that many judges' eyes have been opened. Although the Supreme Court, led by the traitor Van Loon, still hesitates and trembles, the courts of appeal and county courts have awakened. [. . .]

VOLKSCHE GEEST (THE "SPIRIT OF THE VOLK")

A boy who was sent to Ommen because he had listened to an English broadcast was returned home "for good behavior," with the information that from now on he was allowed to listen to the radio continually. Both his eardrums had been pierced.

Het Parool. May 28, 1943

NEWS IN BRIEF

[. . .] The anti-Jewish measures are being multiplied. We have before mentioned the beginning of measures against "mixed marriages." Since then, we have learned that the main lines of their regulation are as follows: the Jewish partner in the mixed marriage is given the choice between sterilization and deportation to Poland. Sterilizations are to be conducted in the Central Israelitic Hospital by German physicians with the aid of Jewish nurses, who will be forced to render their services in this abject work. The expenses of the procedure must be borne by the Jews. [. . .]

Trouw. June 3, 1943

[. . .] It is shameful how small the number is of those who have been truly moved in their soul by this war, who sense what is at stake, and who are prepared to sacrifice everything in this . . . struggle. The majority do not know the readiness to sacrifice without which not a single great victory can be gained. [. . .]

Radios

Let no one hand in his radio voluntarily. It is better to wait until eventually it is picked up.

Do not follow the advice to "turn in an old appliance." We deny the enemy the right of confiscation, on the basis of article 46 of the Geneva Convention, which says: "Private property cannot be confiscated."

If you have an old radio, do not display it, so that in case of seizure not even a thing of little value falls into the enemy's hands.

Hide your good radio in such a way that you can continue to listen, and see to it that you have it within reach on the day of reversal. Accept the watchword: not a single appliance for the enemy.

Recap

[. . .] Initially, many of us understood that the request for an *Ausweis* [written permission given by German officials] in order to escape work in Germany or the status of prisoner of war was wrong. Hence, when the population was granted the opportunity to acquire such an *Ausweis*, large numbers of people refused to do so. It was understood that requesting an *Ausweis* for those whom the Germans wanted to keep here opened the way for the deportation of others.

It was understood that applying for the *Ausweis* did not mean anything else than officially entering one's name. And every form of reporting was and is wrong. One must not volunteer to stick one's head into the noose.

Suddenly this proper attitude departed. The populace has begun to suffer a mania to secure *Ausweise*.

The massive resistance, the national front concentrated in the one act of refusal to go because it is immoral to go, dissolved into a collection of clever little individual tricks. That is how a stampede came about of hundreds and thousands of persons to get hold of a piece of paper in order to save one's bacon.

[. . .] Glory to those who stand their ground even now, especially now, with respect to the *Ausweise* . . .

Two Thousand of the Eleven Thousand

Of the 11,000 professional military men who should have reported for transport as prisoners, fewer than 2,000 showed up in Amersfoort.

Transport took place in cattle cars that were nailed shut and only partly equipped for human use.

Who is next?

Let no proud Dutchman allow himself to be taken away like that.

Trouw. June 3, 1943

The Suffering of Jews in the Netherlands

The Germans have taken an intensified interest in the Jews. This is in accord with the communication of the Rijkscommissaris, who came out with the statement the other day that "this very year" the Jewish question here would be solved.

[. . .] The *Hetze* [Jew-baiting] exploded again when after the call for Jews in Amsterdam to report on May 20 only 980 of the 14,000 showed up. Measures clamped down on those in possession of a *sperstempel* [a stamp on one's identity card exempting the bearer from deportation] as a result of their work for the Jewish Council, and half of the existing exemptions from deportation were withdrawn, including those of German Jews residing in the Netherlands. A new order to report by May 25 again did not yield the desired result.

Thereupon, the maniacs began their hunt on the night of May 25 and continued the following day. The Jewish quarters were barricaded, and only guarded streetcars with their doors shut could pass through . . . In this manner they go on hunting, all hell breaks loose, and the suffering among Jews is indescribable.

[. . .] The satanic rage is never ending. In Westerbork 100 Jews of mixed marriages, with or without children, were put to the choice: either Poland or sterilization. Forty-seven chose Poland, while the other 53 chose what in our opinion was worse—sterilization.

When in addition we consider the measure, promulgated in defiance of earlier promises, directing Jews who had become Christian to

Westerbork, we see ever more the Jewish suffering of which the depth is unfathomable.

Deeply troubled, we watch all this take place in our Christian Netherlands. To what judgment will they have to submit themselves who still call themselves Dutchmen and who participate in these things!

THE WAR

Whoever makes an inventory of the Allies' military harvest this past month will surely run out of space! The Russians concentrated their armies for the summer offensive, especially on the central and northern sector of the front, and at the same time began an air offensive against German traffic junctions. The Americans landed on Attu, and thereupon they will no doubt begin the attack on Kiska, which is another of the Aleutian Islands, where excellent airfields will provide the conditions for large-scale air attacks on the islands of Japan. At night the Royal Air Force and during the day the American bombers cover one German war industry after the other with bombs . . . But still more important than all this is the victory in Africa.

More quickly and more completely than anyone had dared to guess, the Allied armies in North Africa have broken the resistance of the enemy and thus fixed him up with a second Stalingrad . . .

Amsterdam, June 6, 1943

Dear Johan,

You'll be mightily surprised to get a letter again from me, but it will be clear to you at once. Friday we had an unexpected visit from our neighbors. Anyway, you will have heard about that. But now comes the reason for writing my letter. I am writing here at my new address, and am well in the J.I.[1] Three of us have a separate room. It's very nice. One of these three is a very well known violinist who has often played for the radio. Naturally we talk about music, and also about our band. We have plans to make music together, I with the clarinet and my roommate with his violin. We do have music— but the clarinet is missing. Now my question is: Would there be a possibility that I could get my clarinet that I played in Oostvoorne? I'll be very happy to pay for it. Now, if you would be kind enough to ask Mr. van der Hor about it, you could tell me. If this could be brought about, it would be wonderful for me. You said that that instrument of mine isn't used now anyway. The question is only whether the society approves. I suppose you might put in a good word for me. I'll take good care of it. In short, do whatever you can. For the rest, there is not much going on here. The neighbors have told me that many people from among you also have to leave. It's very bad.

Now I had better stop again, for I have to go back to my work. So Johan, you will do your best, yes? Thank you very much in advance. Warm regards also to your father and mother and Pietje and Kruina from the three of us, especially from me.

Ben

1. Joodse Invalide, the Jewish Hospital.

Amsterdam, June 19, 1943

Dear Johan and family,

I received your letter last night and read that with my clarinet things just won't come off. It's a great pity, but I can understand it, and, to tell you the truth, I had expected it. I would love to have the instrument that you wrote about, but you will understand that it is too expensive for us. We have been living without income since last year, and who knows how long this has to go on. It's a pity that nothing can be changed about that. But if you run into one that is cheaper, I'll be pleased. It's true, for a good clarinet 100 guilders is not much, but we cannot afford it. For us it is a large expenditure. Everything has remained the same here. Just about every day we have air-raid warnings. But otherwise everything is quiet. I guess that many members of the band have to leave too, right? Now, people, I have to finish, for I am going to eat. So Johan, you know, if you find one in Musica that is cheaper, I'll be pleased. Then we could have an ensemble in our room.

Warm greetings, and we'll see each other, we hope.

Ben

Trouw. June 23, 1943

"HE IS ALL RIGHT"

First Case

Early in the morning, the doorbell awakens an aged couple.

"It's the Dutch Police. Is your son (age 21) at home?"

The son, alerted, quickly hides, and at the door there is some talk back and forth. After this delay, the answer comes: "No."

The house is searched, but the son has disappeared, which nevertheless does not prevent the entire place from being ransacked.

When leaving, the policeman apologizes: "It's an unpleasant time. I can't do anything else."

The father concludes: "He is all right."

Second Case

The only son is a university student and he is called up to sign the loyalty declaration [a document students were to sign if they wanted to continue their study].

He refuses.

The father, a Dutch officeholder, urges him to go ahead and do it, because he should realize: "Your father's livelihood is at risk."

Still the student refuses.

Suddenly, in the midst of the *Standgericht* [ironic reference to German-instituted "legal" measures to deal with opponents, usually by the death penalty], Rauter's order [Johann Rauter was the supreme SS officer in the Netherlands] is delivered: the student should report for the *arbeidsinzet* [obligatory work in Germany].

"Go, report," says the father. "No," says the son.

Packed up and ready, he leaves the house. The father imagines that he is on his way to report. But the son does not do this and, instead, he reports to his *onderduik* [hiding] address.

Would you like ten such cases? Just take a little time and look around you.

Officials use every argument they can muster to persuade youths to get themselves *Ausweise,* and to report: just go to this or that person, "because he is all right."

Parents try to convince their sons, wives their husbands, friends their friends, colleagues their colleagues, not to commit sabotage or do illegal work: "I don't do it either, and I am all right!"

The minister no longer prays for the queen, but "he is all right."

[. . .] A controller gives a ticket to someone who carries to his family vegetables that were destined to go to Germany. "But he is all right."

A mayor grabs radios for the enemy. Okay, we go along, "for he is all right."

A gendarme takes prisoners to the camps of misery in Vught or Ommen. Many are approaching a certain death. On the way, he is accommodating to the prisoners, for "he is all right."

What are we talking about?

They are all "all right," but they all assist the enemy toward his victory—if such a thing were still possible. In any event, they stand in the way of his downfall. They lend support to the illegitimate tyranny; they collaborate in the robbery, they steal our food.

They do it all, for "now you still have someone who is all right, and if I go, you will have a wrong one."

Do you know what the great misery is in this chorus, which everyone sings? It is the fact that everyone is out to save himself, and forgets that we are in the war together.

The one "who is all right" sees to it that he does not get his clothes torn up. But that is not how it should be!

The only one who is truly all right is the one who refuses everything the enemy demands, who does not pass the decision on to someone else, and who follows the order to commit sabotage, courageously and loyally. That person is truly all right!

Amsterdam, July 2, 1943

Dear people,

Fortunately, I can write that all three of us are still healthy, and that we have been saved in spite of the largest *razzia* that ever took place here. We have been exempted from Poland because I work for the Germans. Also my three cousins who are living with us are still here. For the rest, everything is gone. Also my friend Iet who lived with us in the house. It's very sad. There are hardly any Jews left in Amsterdam. I cannot write much now; I'll send a letter along with the bargeman.

Warm regards and until we meet again, also from Father and Mother. Your friend,

Ben

Johan, pass the information on to the neighbors.

Amsterdam, July 6, 1943

Dear Johan and family,

At last, I have another chance to write to you. The tension we have had here in the last few days has been unbearable and indescribable. Now, however, the uncertainty that was the core of it all—whether we had to go, yes or no—is gone. I got myself an *Ausnahmebescheinigung*,[1] because I work for the SS. Also Father and Mother have one, and that means we do not have to be afraid that we'll be "picked up" in the street or at home or with a *razzia*. Of course, we don't know how long something like this will be valid. Our house in the Plantagelaan has been closed up and we are no longer allowed to go there. I don't know where Father and Mother's

address is going to be (at least, not yet). My address is Weesperplein 1, Amsterdam-Central. Also Carla has an *Ausweis*. What a delight it would be for Father and Mother if someday they would get a message from Nan. But now something else. You wrote that Mr. van der Hor had a clarinet (a solo clarinet) for sale. At the time I wrote to you that it was too expensive. However, now I would like to have it. I have the money for it too. Would you people be able to send the instrument to me? To my address! Father will then transmit the money. As soon as possible, please. By parcel post, if it can't be done otherwise. That would be fine. I would very much like to have an instruction book with it, you know, one of the sort I had in the beginning with my instrument. For I am afraid that I won't be able to make much of it anymore. I would also like to have ordinary sheet music with it, if possible. For I don't have music. And obviously, also reeds. In this line nothing can be purchased anymore here. I had better stop, for it is one-thirty and I have to go back to work. So Johan, I suppose you'll write that the instrument will come quickly. Then I'll be happy again. (My cousins are also gone. We are the only ones left now.) Warm regards and the
very best,

    Ben

    1. A certificate of exemption.

Amsterdam, July 20, 1943

Dear Johan and family,

It's quite a while ago that I wrote to you, so I take up the pen again. How are things going with you? With us everything is still unchanged. This moment I am sitting and writing on the roof garden of the "Jewish Invalid." The weather is delightful. It's almost like the beach in Oostvoorne. This is a nice place to tan. I really wonder how Ina is doing (and, not in the last place, how about Kobie!!), and how is Jaap Tieman? I wish I could talk with all of them again one more time. How are things coming with my clar-

inet? Do I get it soon? Will it come along tomorrow? I am so eager
to find out. How long will it take until we can roam about in the
Overbos? Still, things are beginning to get somewhere. We still
haven't heard anything from Nan. He has been gone for almost a
year now. Time surely flies. Do you remember his leaving? Who
could have thought that it would take so long. I still see him going
with his backpack and his blanket roll. And then knowing that you
would never hear anything from him anymore. Do you still see Kees
Bolle from time to time? Tell me, is that evacuation of Oostvoorne
going to take place or not? Nowadays we have air-raid sirens or
warning signals every day. Last Saturday bombs were dropped, and
many living quarters are wrecked. Also a school that was full. Not
full with children!!(???)[1] Father, Mother, and Carla have a room in the
Jewish hospital. I go there every day to the extent the shifts permit
it. I am a doorman now. And I am sitting at the telephone. Johan,
would you please check in Oostvoorne and see whether there is still
a new coat of mine somewhere? If so, would you send it up at the
next occasion? Well, I have run out of demands, and I'll finish with
warm greetings also from Father and Mother. Your friend

    Ben

    1. The question marks and exclamation points imply that the school was
requisitioned and used by Germans.

                          Amsterdam, July 30, 1943
Dear Johan and family,

    It's time to write to you too, for I really feel like writing again.
How are things going with you people in the "hamlet?" I have the
idea that pretty soon I'll be with you again. It's downright unbeliev-
able! Well, it doesn't have to be believable, as long as it is true. Johan,
you can do me a great favor by sending me a few picture postcards
from Oostvoorne. I would very much like to have them in my room.
You know what I have in mind: some beautiful views of our village,
and the dunes, or also the town center. And of course of the station

road!!!¹ Would you mind checking at the neighbors' and finding out whether they still have a photograph of our house? I sometimes long to see our house. I found an old-fashioned film roll here for your father, a Gevaert. It won't expire until 1944. I'll pass it on at the first occasion. How are things with my clarinet? Will I get it before 1950? Or do I have to come pick it up myself? Who are your friends these days, Johan? Do you still see much of Kees Bolle? How are Ina and Kobie and Jaap? I assume you will be advanced in school this year, right? I hope so much to return to school one day. If not to learn, then to talk once again with everybody. I suppose you are going to school swim sessions again. Here, every day is hard work. I am back in the archives. I have to sort out things there. I have no trouble passing the time. How are Pietje and Kruina? Mr. Schipper, can you still get taps to protect shoes? Here they ran out of that sort of thing long ago. I am looking longingly for my clarinet's arrival every day, but nothing has shown up yet. We haven't heard anything from you this week; there is nothing the matter in particular, I hope? I believe I have been asking quite a few questions, when I go down the list. I suppose that the band must have deteriorated quite a bit, now that all military men had to report again. Let us hope that it is only for a little while and that we do not have to face the winter anymore. As to Nan, we still haven't heard or seen anything. Tomorrow I'll have a reproduction made of his picture, the same one you have. The Ortskommandant in Oostvoorne deprived us of our pictures, then, at that time.² The plan to have a few more made never came off, but now I'll see to it. It'll be reproduced from the one Mother has. Recently, the family Kamman came, unexpectedly. That was nice. Also Mrs. Schipper of the bicycle repairman.³ And Piet Willmes⁴ from the village. It surely is a pity that we are no longer living in the Plantage Franschelaan, for that place was so homey. To the extent that homeyness can exist at present. My cousins are also gone. Also transported from Westerbork. This moment, we are sitting in the delightful sun and are writing from the roof terrace of the Jewish Invalid. Just like last time. If you weren't informed better, you would imagine that they wish nothing worse upon us. But now I am really finishing up, for in the meanwhile time has passed, and the sun is moving toward Oostvoorne, and down into the sea. Well, people, I am coming to an end with warm regards and see you!

Ben

Warm greetings also from Father and Mother.

1. The Wessels had their home there.
2. Compare the letter of Oct. 15, 1942.
3. Neighbors on the Station Road in Oostvoorne.
4. Cigar storekeeper in the village.

August 7, 1943

Dear Johan and family,

I received your letter last night, and I'll reply at once (so I am rid of it!). How are you? With us everything is still OK, and let's hope that this is the case with you too. I did pass on the roll of film. Johan, my congratulations on your success in the high school. So now, on to the home stretch. Let us hope that next year is better than this one. For you it wouldn't be pleasant either if by then it has not come to an end yet. Then you too might perhaps have to leave. But fortunately we have not reached that point yet. I read in your letter that you have bought picture postcards. By all means, get as many kinds as you can. That would be nice. At any rate, try to get one of the Stationsweg too. And of course, more views of the village, and of the Overbos, etc. In short, go right ahead and send a whole collection. As long as you let me know at once what it costs. Odd, isn't it, that one can long so much for a village. It seems as though if we ever return, the entire place will have been torn down. Then we can turn on our heels. You people must have kept warm this past winter, when all the camping cabins were burned up in the stoves. What are you going to do now, on your vacation? If you get bored, you may consider visiting me! You are certainly welcome. Is the bandstand of the village gone too? Or is it still there? You know, your letter made me laugh. You wrote: this has been leveled, that is gone, of that nothing is left, and for the rest nothing has changed. That's just like the man who had a headache, and a terrible stomach cramp and pain in his belly, and a toothache on top of it all, and for the rest he felt fine. That's how it is with the village. When I try to imagine what happened, there isn't much left standing. If I read [your letter] right, Kees Bolle has not changed in the least. He has another "reading mania." In earlier days it was the disease of stamp collecting, and now it is something else. Anyway, by all means, give him my regards. I read in your letter that people out there also have *Ausweise*. It is just like here. I have an *Ausweis* too. But after all's said and done, I can no longer make head or tail "aus weis." Now something else, and, to be particular, the clarinet. I read that you need to inquire into the price first. I thought you had already mentioned it: about 100 guilders. So you don't have to write about the price anymore. If it costs about gld. 100, you can go right ahead and send it. Of course, it doesn't matter if it is a bit more or less expensive, as long as it is about that amount. But I can count on it being a solo clarinet, right? I will also get a bit of music with it, and reeds, yes? I surely hope I'll get it soon, for we have a little ensemble, and then I'll be able to play in it. The group consists of 3 violins, one piano, voice, cornet, viola, and then—in thought—a clarinet. We, or rather, they played on the radio here in the building. We have a radio installation here, and a microphone, and our own studio, and we transmit from our own studio to the rooms with the people. That's nice. Now I see that I filled another two pages, and I know that you folks are not all that patient with me, so I am finishing with warm greetings, and so long, from all of us,

Ben

Amsterdam, August 19, 1943

Dear Johan and family,

I suppose you will also have received the tragic report of the arrest of Father and Mother.[1] Yes, my friend, you don't know how happy you are, although you may not realize it. Perhaps it seems to you as if I put on the airs of an eighty-year-old, but I mean it, honestly. For the rest, there is nothing special here. Except that here in the building we are up to our neck in work. The surgical patients from the hospital where Father used to be are all here with us. Also the contagious diseases. All the other sick people have been sent on. You will understand that things are not easy for me. It is not easy for me, as a boy of almost 17, to be all by myself in a large, strange city. But let's hope that it is only for a little while. You had better not look at my handwriting, for I am very much in a hurry. I have to go back to work in a minute. Schipper, thank you very much for the shoe taps! What do they cost? Thanks to you also, Johan, for the cards. But by all means, do tell me what I owe you. You will understand that under the circumstances I give up on the idea of the clarinet. I would have no wish for something like that anywhere near me, let alone to play it. Well, people, I really have to return to my work now. Warm wishes, and so long,

Ben

1. At the occasion of this arrest, Carla was rescued (see the introduction), a rescue that Ben could not mention because of censorship.

Trouw. August 19, 1943

PERSEVERANCE UNTIL THE END

Unmistakably, the end of our tribulation is in sight. No one can say how long this last stretch will be, but it is certain that terror will increase to the extent the tyrant feels harassed . . . The chaos of misery and mourning that these evildoers have brought over us has no parallel in modern history. But the end is not here yet.

The brazen-faced plunder and the systematic hunt for human material goes on with intense stubbornness. One injustice is piled on top of another, a human life counts for less than our worthless money, even children (Jewish children) are the defenseless prey of these bandits.

We have no illusions. A still harder fate is in store for us. It is good to count on it and be prepared, so that we can take the beatings with the resiliency of steel. For woe unto us if we became accustomed to injustice, if no indignation flared up in us at the report of each shameful violation, if we weakened in our spiritual resistance.

Many among us have never known that spiritual resistance, but only know how to bow down deeper at each new act of violence. Their lust for self-preservation is the only measuring rod of their comportment.

Praise God, there are also many whose spirit is unbroken, and who are prepared to challenge each atom of the enemy's power until the bitter end. They know that their stance determines the inner worth of our people. Their unbroken spirit of resistance is the anvil on which the tyrant breaks one hammer after another.

[. . .] They do not ask what the others are doing, they do not get mired in discussions of whether this is still possible or that is worth the trouble. They act where they are called to act.

Often they stand alone. Sometimes they are not understood by those around them, or are even opposed, but they persist, knowing that in their struggle no compromise is acceptable.

This conviction usually has its origin in the complete surrender of the Christian faith. The Christian knows that now more than ever faith must be manifest in works, and in full confidence he leaves the results of his obedience to God's commandment in the hands of his heavenly Father.

To the extent that our resistance has this spiritual background, it is of lasting value, for the future as well as the present. Even now we know with certainty that each refusal in principle of the simple laborer to let himself become part of the enemy's war machine is of great, lasting significance. [. . .]

Amsterdam, September 6, 1943

Dear Johan and family,

There has been a bit more delay in writing than I intended. In the first place, many thanks for the package! It was !!?—here they would say: something good to kiss. That's how it was, but especially good to eat. The rest came in handy. As you knew, I was itching for it. I also received your warmhearted letter. Yes, you know how it is. It is not easy to write about things like this. It isn't easy for me either. How are all of you? And Pietje and Kruina? The package arrived open and torn up. It hadn't been packed well at all. I am not writing this for myself, of course. I also received the photograph of Nan and myself. This, however, is not the one I meant. I meant the picture of Nan by himself. I think that the neighbors have one. Would you mind asking them? Johan, will you check for a picture of our house? And a picture postcard of the Station Road? Perhaps I am bothering you a great deal, but you understand that I really long for pictures. Especially now. How is the family Kamman? Give my greetings to them especially. Let us hope that things won't last so long anymore, and that we'll all see each other again in good health. Johan, will you answer soon? The more mail, the happier I am. All right, people, I am coming to an end again with warm greetings, and wishes for seeing each other. Your friend,

Ben

Will you please check whether there is still a suit of Nan's? If possible, I would like to have it.

Amsterdam, September 26, 1943

Dear family Stolk,[1]

I don't have to spell out how I liked hearing from you. I was very happy with your letter. We still think back to Oostvoorne nostalgically, to the time we had there, so pleasant, and especially so quiet compared to the present. Living out here the difference becomes so obvious. For us here, one day is like every other day. There is always the same fear and misery. And again and again the thought: where are Mother and Father and Nan? Mother and Father also left for Germany, as you most probably know. I haven't heard anything more from them. Being all by myself in a large city like Amsterdam, I have no family left, and so there isn't much fun to it anymore.

That's why I am so eternally grateful to hear from our people with whom we have always been friends. Last week, the family

Gazon[2] was also sent on to Poland. The whole family, Mrs. and Mr. Gazon, and Liesje. Awful. What misery the war causes us. How are things with you on the Straatweg? Does everything go on there as usual? I also am very busy, and I am happy about it, for then time passes more quickly. Anyhow, let's keep our spirits up. Perhaps everything will still turn out all right with us. Let's hope that the war will be over soon, and that all of us can return to our own dwellings. Well, people, warm greetings, so long, and once again many thanks!

B. L. Wessels

B. Wessels, Weesperplein 1, Amsterdam

1. The addressee of this letter is not identified. According to Johan Schipper, the letter may have been put into the wrong envelope.

2. A Jewish family from Brielle.

Amsterdam, September 26, 1943

Dear Johan and family,

I am off duty at the moment, so I have a good opportunity to sit and write at ease. How are things in Oostvoorne? As to myself, I am still OK. We did have quite a day last week Friday, but by now that's forgiven and forgotten. No, I doubt whether that day can really be forgiven. And I don't think I'll ever forget it either, although that's what I wrote. I narrowly escaped being stuck in Westerbork or Poland by now. However, all I can do now is wait for the next shock. To be perfectly frank, I am bored stiff after my work nowadays. Actually, that's easy to understand. My girlfriend is also gone now, so I haven't got anything anymore. I did have a girlfriend here. A girl of my age, and she used to keep me company in the evening. Alas, that is also finished now. Last week I got a very nice letter from Ina Pleit. I was very happy with it. That same day I got a letter from the family Kamman. Both these letters arrived together with your "epistle," so I had quite a bit to read—a delight for me. When shall I be walking about in Oostvoorne again? Johan, you usually know things. When will the war be over? Anyhow, before we are that far, it looks as if I'll have to go on a little trip. The future doesn't look rosy at all. We have been given a very different assignment here in the house. Very different work. It's going to be even busier in the building. How are your friends doing? Do you still see them? What grade is Maarten Heindijk[1] in now? I heard that Jaap Tieman is taking the course for engineers.[2] So he also has to go through contortions to be safe. How is Nel Lobs and how is Kees Bolle (and families)? If possible, give them my greetings. And don't forget Jaap Tieman! I still hope to talk with you people myself again, in a while, in Oostvoorne. But it's got to happen soon. Otherwise it might be too late for me. All right, let's think of the song they're singing all day here in the house: "Come on, come on, not that gloom." Well, Johan, I'm ending up again in the old way. Warm greetings and a firm handshake, and so long, your

Ben

1. A classmate in Hellevoetsluis.
2. At the technical high school in Brielle.

Het Parool. September 27, 1943

CONCENTRATION CAMPS:
WHERE THE NAZIS APPLY THEIR *IDEALS*

We are able at last to offer the reader an account of the concentration camps that is based not on "rumors" and "gruesome stories" but on the author's personal experience. All doubt as to "whether such things can be true" dissolves. They are true. Learn how the National Socialist scum treats human beings. Renew your spirit of resistance against a system that is so unworthy of man as to make *all words fail.*

The concentration camp is one of the most characteristic institutions of the National Socialist state, a community of guards and prisoners that can be viewed as the National Socialist model of social life. The National Socialist dream for the future of state and society is already realized in the concentration camp. National Socialist conceptions of right, duty, labor, discipline, and order have here been applied perfectly.

Early in 1933, when the large landowners of Germany, in collaboration with a number of industrialists and bankers, handed over power to the party of Hitler, concentration camps were soon set up in all parts of the Dritte Reich. Everyone who disagreed with the new government was placed in such a model institute for the education of National Socialist citizens. Since then, the most reputed camps have probably been Buchenwald, Sachsenhausen, Neu Gammen, Dachau, and Mauthausen. Cautiously, those in the know estimate the number of Germans who found their death there from 1933 to 1939 at half a million.

Since German National Socialism began its campaign for the conquest of Europe in 1939, a large number of new concentration camps have been opened in Germany and the territories occupied by the German Wehrmacht. Millions of Russians, Poles, Jews, Czechs, Yugoslavs, and others have been brought to them and killed. They number probably between four and six million. Most often, a concentration camp is situated in moorland, in a forest, or somewhere in the mountains. It is enclosed by high barbed-wire barriers. Sometimes electrically charged wires are also installed around the camp. Some camps are surrounded by a deep moat. Around the outer fencing, at distances of at most a hundred meters, little towers are built. On each, an SS guard with a machine gun keeps watch day and night. Nevertheless, occasionally prisoners try to escape. If they are caught, it is the end for them; before the entire troop they are beaten to death or hanged. Throughout the camp at various points, machine guns are set up.

Prisoners are shod with clogs. They wear prison clothes with conspicuous stripes. Their heads are shaved. They are lodged in barracks with iron bunk beds stacked in threes. Most often, three or four people lie side by side in two beds shoved together, because there is never enough space. The whole place swarms with body lice, and people scratch themselves ceaselessly. The general lack of hygiene makes scabies rampant. Most often each barrack has its own toilet. Toilet facilities consist of some ten privies arranged next to each other, so that everything is done in public. In this manner, National Socialism puts an end to petty bourgeois individualism.

Often during the night the running water is turned off, so that the toilets cannot be flushed. What this does to the atmosphere in a barrack of some two to four hundred men may be imagined.

Generally, the prisoners must go to bed at nine in the evening. At 4:00 AM they get up. In wintertime this occurs one hour later. When the daylight lasts longer, and especially when it is warm, no one is able to sleep before eleven; hence everyone suffers from chronic lack of sleep. The night has its disagreeable surprises. An SS man may suddenly rush into the barrack. This may happen, for instance, because a trash can was left outside. He compels the prisoners to rise and to run up and down the dormitory, to crouch underneath the beds, or to do other exercises. After all, sport and physical training keep people fit. National Socialism knows and practices this.

In the morning there is no food. The only thing that is distributed is a cup of brown liquid. Then at 5:30 there is the morning roll call. Barrack by barrack has to line up. In accordance with German custom, roll call takes place under uninterrupted shouting and swearing. *Ordnung muss sein* [there must be order]. Following the roll call, everyone marches at the double to his *Arbeitskommando* [work section]. Virtually every concentration camp has its *Kommando* for woodcutters, quarriers, sand diggers, potato peelers, and so on. Prisoners who are designated to keep the toilets clean form the *Abortreinigungskommando*. So all work is organized along military lines. Hence there is also a trash-can *Kommando* marching in closed ranks, rigidly executing the loudly screamed orders. During the work, which lasts sometimes only ten hours, but often fourteen or even sixteen hours a day, SS men with cudgels are everywhere present; they see to it that no one rests for a moment. The least SS man represents the authority of the state in the camp. Therefore everyone must take off his cap when such a mighty representative passes by. Keep in mind that this representative is fully entitled to beat you ferociously. More roll calls follow in the afternoon and evening. At those occasions the corpses are brought in on wheelbarrows and the SS-Arbeitsführer [work leader] clicks his heels and gives the Hitler salute and reports to the Rapportführer [report leader]: *"Drei Häftlinge auf der Flucht erschossen!"* [three prisoners shot while fleeing].

In some camps nutrition is not particularly bad. In most, however, hunger is the rule. Whoever is able to stand the heavy labor, the lack of sleep, and the torture, and the lack of food for three months is still bound to lose 20 to 40 kilos in weight. In most camps the inmate population becomes extinct four times per year. Consequently, one of the German camps has a crematorium operating with four ovens under full power, day and night.

Every prisoner who notices a comrade's transgression of one of the many rules must report the matter at once to the SS. If he neglects to do so he is just as punishable as the transgressor. Everyone is a policeman and an informer with respect [to] his neighbor. Each person watches, spies on, and betrays his fellow creature. Whoever doesn't do so is a traitor. This is how the camp teaches National Socialist morality.

The transgressor of rules is punished. One of the more innocent penalties is to "stand at the gate for a week." Then the punished man as a rule receives no food; during all hours outside work time, hence his "free time," he must stand at attention at the inside gate of the camp, in heat, rain, snow, or freezing temperature, and continually take off and replace his cap for the SS men who are rushing in and out. Occasionally someone must stand at the gate for an entire month. This leads to complete exhaustion, and often disease or death. At the center of the concentration camp there is usually a large prison. Whoever ends up there will be *"fertig gemacht,"* put to death, within a few days. Mauthausen had a man by the name of Etlinger as its prison commander. Etlinger saw fit to make prisoners entrusted to him "fertig" within one day. At present, he is employed in the concentration camp of Vught, where he will take up his old specialty as soon as the prison that is now being built is completed.

For the rest, each German camp has the "buck" and the "pole."

The buck is a high bench; a man is laid facedown on it and tied in place; in that position, he receives 25 or 50 lashes with a cudgel or a steel wire. With this treatment the wretch's bottom is beaten to a bloody pulp. There are those who cannot stand this and who perish. But of course, they are the unhealthy or weaklings. For such folk there is no place in National Socialist society.

The pole is an instrument of torture that makes one think of Golgotha. With his hands tied behind his back, the prisoner is put on a table against the high pole that is firmly planted in the earth. From the top of the pole hangs a strap that is fixed to the prisoner's tied wrists. Then the table is pulled away. The fall jerks the victim's arms up and the shock wrenches them from their sockets. He remains hanging. Once in Dachau they let 17 people hang that way for two hours. After that, two were still alive.

Concentration camp Sachsenhausen has been established in the former Olympic village. Where at one time youthful athletes from all over the world competed with each other, now the children of French, Czech, Polish, and Russian mothers are crushed under the Nazi boot. A two-kilometer road runs through this camp. It has been paved with human bones. The Third Reich has no lack of this material. The problem of overpopulation in the camp has been solved in a sober and businesslike fashion. The sick receive a cyanide injection. Twice a week the camp physician makes his rounds through the *Revier,* the hospital barrack. Everyone knows what this visit means. The doctor points to some fifty patients. A prisoner who functions as secretary takes down their numbers. Fifteen minutes later those written down are called to the ambulance. They go, and know that this is their last walk on earth. The ambulance is the place of the camp physician and his aides, a pair of nurses. The syringe does its job. The cards can be removed from the card system. Somewhere in a village in Czechoslovakia or in a French town a woman cannot answer her children's question why their daddy does not write anymore.

In the winter of 1941–42, prisoners were submitted to experiments to determine the limits of human endurance under circumstances like those of the inclement Russian climate. To this end some ten prisoners were dressed well, poorly, or not at all, tied up, and placed in the snow. Some were given good food, some bad food, some no food at all. Their temperature was taken regularly. In this way statistics were gathered, and when the test persons had all died, the needed information had been acquired. National Socialism spares no pains in the conquest of scientific challenges.

This appears to be the case also in Mauthausen. In barrack I of the camp a brothel has been set up. In exchange for 75 pfennig, prisoners can pay a visit. Some of the prisoners can go in free of charge; they have been sterilized. But interest in the institution is not overwhelming. At certain moments, visitors must demonstrate what sexual feats they are capable of in the presence of the camp commander, the camp physician, and other interested persons. When it comes to science, National Socialism does indeed overcome all barriers. For the rest, Mauthausen is one of the worst camps. This is the place where Jews arrested during the February Strike of 1941 in Amsterdam were disposed of. The wretches were bound back to back and driven up on a rock 60 meters high. From there they were chased down into a quarry. In this place tens of thousands of lives were destroyed in a short span of time. And what could not be done fast enough here was taken to Mauthausen's satellite, the nearby camp of Gusen. There, tasks were undertaken with even more energy. At an appropriate moment a good load of dynamite would be exploded in the quarry.

This yielded always 200 corpses minimum, and sometimes as many as 400. The inventive National Socialist in charge at the time was Hauptsturmführer Chmiliefsky. Nowadays this man is commander of the concentration camp of Vught.

In the course of the war, liquidation of imprisoned opponents and enemies has been made significantly more efficient. The process, for which the technical term is *"umlegen"* [kill, "waste"], has been conducted for quite a while now in gas chambers, which are built in all the camps. Such a chamber seems to be a shower room. A large number of people are brought into it naked. This has the advantage that afterward the corpses can be cremated at once, without the trouble of having to be undressed. The procedure is simple. The doors close and the faucets open up. Fifteen minutes later, the corpse commando enters and drags out the victims. In the camp of Auschwitz tens of thousands of Poles, Jews, and Russians have been killed. Half a year ago, the gas chamber, which used to have a capacity of 200, was enlarged considerably, so that at present 1,000 can get in at the same time. In the gas chamber of Neu Gammen (near Hamburg) many Dutchmen have been killed.

In this latest German war of conquest, all countries liberated by the Wehrmacht from the Jewish-Bolshevistic-Plutocratic system have been provided with their own concentration camps. Apart from camps for Jews, such camps exist in our country at Ommen, Amersfoort, and Vught. Although in our country hundreds of people have been murdered in camps, we must establish the fact that the slaughter here is in no way comparable in size to that in Germany itself. The largest number of dead was reached in November 1942 in Amersfoort, when among about 1,500 inmates 78 people died. This took place under the responsibility of three men whose names one might do well to remember: Hauptsturmführer Heinrich, Untersturmführer Stöver, and Hauptscharführer Berg. The camp of Vught, which was put to use on January 15, 1943, initially had days on which 10 to 15 deaths occurred. However, in recent times the situation there has improved.

In fact, a general improvement has come about in the regime of German concentration camps. It is related to the new induction of camp inmates as much as possible to productive labor for the benefit of the German war effort. For instance, in Vught prisoners nowadays produce radios and electric razors at an assembly line under the guidance of the Philips Factories. In many German camps prisoners work to produce such things as ammunition and parts for airplanes. Obviously, prisoners who are at work for the war industry need to be treated differently from prisoners who are merely kept busy by having them ride wheelbarrows with sand from left to right and right to left. It almost seems to begin to dawn on Berlin that the vanquished nations can hardly be won over for "the battle against the Asian hordes" as long as the sons of those nations are tortured, starved, and killed in concentration camps. Recently, supervisory committees from Berlin suddenly enter the camps; their task is to make sure what goes on is not too barbaric. In addition to this, the lower ranks of camp guards are beginning to realize that this war is going to end with Hitler's defeat, so that most Rottenführer and Unterscharführer do not show a burning desire on the eve of the threatening final account to increase their burden of gruesome deeds. Hence the prisoners in Vught have come to call their camp "the sanatorium." This does not change the fact that an unlucky inmate can still have a few teeth knocked out of his mouth.

The other day one prisoner was battered so severely that one of his eardrums was destroyed. And when a group of prisoners, having heard that [Benito] Mussolini [had] abdicated, were caught singing patriotic songs during their work, they were given punishment drills for two and a half hours in their free time in the evening, whereby rolling over the ground, deep knee bends, jogs, and *"hinlegen und aufstehen"* [lying down and getting up] alternate until a state of complete exhaustion is reached. At the occasion, the Hauptscharführer, a fanatic Nazi, hurled these words at his victims:

"Don't imagine that the war is over. It is only about to begin for real. And if one day we have to leave, we'll first let the machine guns play over the camp!"

But such matters are details and of little importance. The main thing is that all concerned should realize that Germany is at war for Christendom, for west European civilization, and for the preservation of occidental culture.

The conditions and events in the concentration camps present the best proof of this.

POLITICAL PARTIES AFTER THE WAR

In wartime, power is yielded to only a few leaders, whose ideas tend toward a military style. And inevitably, many people begin to think of dictatorship as a form of government desirable also in time of peace. Even among us, the ranks of those who have waved aside all the "fiddling about" of parliaments are not thin. They now assert their conception of a "strong man" who will put an end to "the bickering of political parties." That man by himself alone will govern— of course as a "good Dutchman" and "democratically." We have even seen plans drawn up by countrymen who truly mean well for their fatherland, yet whose grasp on the demands of the time does not reach beyond banishing the "influence of the people" as a most undesirable factor and a threat. These thinkers parrot fascists of all feather in their talk of "the misery of the 53 parties." Although they would not like to divest themselves of the honorific "democrat," they do make a plea for a constitutional arrangement in which a parliament would at best be salvaged in a weak advisory capacity.

It will do no harm to oppose some considerations to such thinking. These considerations compel us to accept a party structure for governing . . .

With regard to its political side, democracy allows everyone to enunciate his principles, to unite with others of the same mind, and through such unity to bring the shared principles into practice. Political power rests on the basis of opinions held by a majority. The minority continues to present its views and to strive toward majority status. Implied in the whole process is the recognition of the equality of all citizens.

This is an equality of worth, of dignity, and absolutely must not be confused with mere equality in the sense of sameness. Only the scholar in the ivory tower, who lacks a sense of reality, forgets that people are entirely unequal in disposition and ability. However, there is no conflict at all between the inequality of human abilities, which forms the foundation on which the social division of functions ought to rest, and the equality in value. Above all, determining the direction of government is a matter of moral judgment, a question of what is allowed and what shall happen. The least educated is just as much called to answer that question as the most educated, the destitute as much as the wealthy, the simple soul as much as the person in authority. Each one is *called*, which does not mean that any one is *obliged* to come up with an answer! Compulsory voting, of the sort we knew in the Netherlands of the past, is as absurd as it is undemocratic. It is absurd, as society cannot expect anything good to come from one who "judges" because he must rather than wishes to judge. It is undemocratic, as freedom includes the freedom not to do something. If a man is forced to pass judgment on a public matter, he is as unfree as one who is forced by a dictator to keep silent.

It is a fact gleaned from experience that our views as to what should occur in society vary in accordance with our social group and the spiritual circle in which we move. Dictatorship takes no interest in this fact, for the dictator cuts all knots without heeding the existence of dissenters, whether they form a majority or a minority. In a democracy, the ruling majority's view determines how decisions will be carried through. But each decision remains subject to the critique of the opponent . . . Democracy is always more difficult than dictatorship. This is precisely the secret of its superior strength . . .

[. . .] A democracy without parties is as impossible as a dictatorship without concentration camps . . .

Trouw. October 1943

PLACE OF HONOR

In the past month a number of executions have again taken place. Their purpose was to frighten and intimidate the Dutch population. In Assen, on September 20, ten splendid men were shot down. Nineteen courageous comrades followed them in death on October 1st.

They are not the only ones who sealed their love for their country with their lives. Many more death sentences are executed than we read about in the papers. We remember also those who were dragged from their homes and shot without any legal process . . .

RAZZIA ON JEWS IN AMSTERDAM

In the night of September 28–29, another *razzia* burst forth upon the last few thousands of Jews left in Amsterdam. At midnight, the Grüne Polizei began their horrible work in collaboration with the Dutch police. That same day some thousands of Jews were sent on to Vught and Westerbork.

This time the attack was aimed at those who possessed the *"Sperr"* stamp [which seemed to guarantee safety from persecution]: initially, it could be obtained as a favor; later, it cost thousands of guilders or an exchange of diamonds. In the months preceding this *razzia*, those who held the stamps had been moved to Amsterdam East. That is where the hunt could now take place with greater ease.

Another group attacked in this *razzia* was the remaining part of the Jewish Council, including among others hospital staff. Among these were also the presidents of the Jewish Council, Mr. Asscher and Professor Cohen. We hardly need to state that patients of the hospitals concerned were among the victims.

Wednesday, September 29, the new Jewish year 7704 began. Another testimony to "the subtle Germanic spirit"; they chose the Jewish New Year's Eve for these atrocities.

In the Gooi region, in Huizen, Naarden, Bussum, and elsewhere, Dutch police lent themselves to cooperate in picking up the last Jews . . .

That night many Jews committed suicide.

Het Parool. October 30, 1943

The Real Jewish Problem

Some time ago we could still say that the Netherlands did not have a Jewish problem. And to the extent some thought it existed, they expressed anti-Semitism. No Jewish problem existed, but only a problem of anti-Semites.

At present, almost three years later, one can no longer write that there is no Jewish problem. On the contrary, it is the most urgent problem of the occupied territories — but in an altogether different sense than the sense in which the anti-Semite uses the term.

[. . .] What has befallen the hundreds of thousands of Jewish Dutchmen is totally incomparable with the suffering of any other group of Dutchmen. Anyone else — be he laborer, doctor, student — who utters a complaint should humble himself in shame when he considers how petty, how insignificant his burden is next to the fate that has engulfed the Jews in the last few years.

Thank God, much is done to lighten their burden. The long list of people the German police still search for contains some tens of thousands of Jewish Dutchmen, and there are thousands more, unlisted, who have escaped the German measures. They went into hiding or fled south past the border.

They have been able to do all this only with the help of innumerable non-Jewish compatriots. However, exactly in connection with such help a mentality has arisen among some Dutchmen that bears the dangerous seeds of anti-Semitism. Stories have circulated during the past half year about individuals who were "betrayed" by a Jew or who got into trouble because of a Jew who "squealed."

[. . .] On the whole, the non-Jewish Dutchmen who try to leave, who go into hiding, or get into trouble with the Germans, form a very select group as to courage and character. After all, the weaklings, the cowards, and all immoral characters see to it that they do not end up in such situations. With the Jews, however, . . . the cowards too, the immoral characters too, have to make the attempt to escape from the Germans, if they do not want to submit to an inevitable death. As a result, they must live far above their means with respect to courage and character. Imagine that a whole city needed to go into hiding, with all its inhabitants in all gradations of good and evil, strength and weakness. Those who tried to help them would have the same experiences as they do now with part of the Jews who are being helped.

[. . .] If one is a good swimmer, he does not let another man drown because there might be some risk attached to the attempt to save him (often because of the clumsiness of the one being saved).

It is incomprehensible that someone who does not count himself among the followers of Himmler refuses to lend a hand to another human being when the other is Jewish, while rendering help to someone else who is not a Jew. Such a person stands condemned like any ordinary anti-Semite, because of his senseless generalizing, his complete lack of critical thought, and his ignorance of the most elementary rule of justice and law: one must not hit one person for the wrong another person has perpetrated.

Westerbork, November 3, 1943

Dear Johan and family,

Finally I have a chance to send a sign of life also to you. How are all of you? I am doing well. I have already been here for a month. But I did not have the opportunity to write. How have things been going on with you? Please, do answer some time if you feel like it.

Give my regards to your friends. If you have a torch, a (flat) flash-light for me, I'll be grateful. Well, friends, warm greetings, and so long,

Ben

afz. Benj. Wessels
28-9-'26

Barak 69 Westerbork
Hooghalen O. (Dr.)

November 17, 1943

Dear Johan and family,

In the first place, I thank you for your letter, which I received 5 days ago. I read that you are still all right. The same is the case with me. I also read that you will send me a flashlight. You do have to watch out that you don't enclose any letter or postcard in the pack-ages. It doesn't matter if you put in blank postcards or postal paper. Nothing is supposed to be written on them. Also, the package is not allowed to be heavier than 2 kilograms. Do pay attention to that. I cannot write many particulars. I have to work hard every day. Johan, if you would have a way to get jackboots for me, size 42, I would be very grateful. If so, do send them registered, also shoe polish and wax, and laces. Only if it is possible! We are walking in the mud here all day, so you get filthy, as you'll understand. If you send packages, by all means, register them! If possible, also bread. That is very wel-come. Well, friends, warm greetings also to others and at school, your friend Ben

AFZ. Benj. Wessels
28-9-26
Bar. 69
Lager Westerbork
Post Hooghalen-Drente

December 1, 1943

Dear Johan,

At last, I can write something again. How are all of you? In the
very first place, I have to thank you for the letter and the picture
postcard. I was enormously happy especially with the picture postcard. I am sure you can imagine that. Of course I am bowled over
that you are doing your best to get some things done for me. Last
night I got the little package that had the flashlight. As you know,
that came in handy. Give my warm regards to Mr. Schoenmaker and
congratulate him on his safe return home. Keep in mind that from
now on you are not allowed to write letters anymore, but have to
use only the reply form attached to this paper. Packages, however,
are permitted. So I am looking forward to the reply form from you
soon. With me out here, everything is still OK, as you must have no-
ticed. How are your mother and father? Maybe you can still get a
pair of goggles there. They are indispensable here. Well, friends, I
have to finish here, for my paper is filled. So I do expect a few lines
in return from you soon. Warm greetings, so long, and the best
wishes, Ben

> Absender: Benjamin Wessels
> Baracke: 69 geboren: 28-9-'26
> LAGER WESTERBORK
> Hooghalen Oost

Het Parool. December 18, 1943

[The sonnet of the following selection came to be recited by many.
Its fame rested not only on the author's reputation or on the fact that
he died at the hands of the enemy. Rather, the poem kindled the
spirit of many in despair. To a modern audience, its style — only ap-
proximated in the prose rendering — is a reminder that the time of

the war was itself part of a very different general era with very different modes of expression than our own.]

Last spring, the poet Jan Campert was killed in a German concentration camp. Below, we print one of his sonnets. For obvious reasons
this poem was not allowed to appear in his last book, *Sonnets for
Cynara*.

REBEL, MIJN HART.

Rebel, mijn hart, gekerkerd en geknecht,
die aan de tralies van den al-dag rukt,
weest om uw tijdlijk lot geenszins bedrukt,
al zijn de kluisters hard, de muren hecht.
Want in den aanvang werd het u voor-zegd
dat het aan enkelen steeds is gelukt
het juk te breken dat hun schouders drukt,
laat dus niet af maar vecht en vecht en vecht.
Breekt uit en blaast de dove sintels aan
die zijn verdoken onder rookend puin;
vaart storm-gelijk over den lagen tuin,
die Holland heet: slaat dood'lijk toe en snel
opdat het kwaad schrikk'lijk zal ondergaan,
o hart, mijn hart, o bloedroode rebel.

[MY HEART, REBEL!

Arise, my imprisoned and enslaved heart,
You who are trying to tear down the bars that are ever around you.
Don't be dismayed by the fate you are to suffer only for a while,
No matter how hard the shackles and how impenetrable the walls.

At the beginning you were given the prophecy
That some shall succeed and cast off the yoke of oppression.
Therefore, persevere in your fight.

Break away and stir up the fire
That is hidden under the smoldering ruins.
Blow like a storm over the low garden
Of Holland, deal deadly blows, so that the evil now ruling
supreme will perish.]

[A gradual shift is noticeable in the bulk of the underground publications. Attention is turning to how things should be after the war. In this context, the subject of the Dutch East Indies inevitably arises. Concern over the fate of the Jews and the subject of the concentration camps does not disappear. Nevertheless, one must take note of the fact that now, by the end of 1943, the Germans had completed their seizure of Dutch Jews.]

Trouw. December 1943

THE SPIRITUAL RESPONSIBILITY OF THE NETHERLANDS TOWARD INDIA

[In accordance with general usage in the Dutch of the time, "India" referred to the Dutch East Indies. Ideas about a free and independent Indonesia were slow in developing. The tone of the article from which the following fragments are quoted is typical of the period and was not restricted to the admittedly right-wing circles of *Trouw.* Obviously, the text is very patronizing. But at the same time, a change of attitude is noticeable: the writer realizes that the postwar relationship to "India" must be something new.]

In these times, when we begin to consider the coming reunion of the Netherlands and India, our thoughts tend to dwell on political and economic dilemmas. We realize that at the great moment when our tricolor flies again over Batavia [the old Dutch name for Jakarta], a rush of problems will advance upon us. We shall have to deal with those problems one by one, in perfect calm and wisdom. More than ever before, the central issue is no longer what we can gain from India, but what we must be, and are allowed to be, for India. For we will see our own role not primarily as principal investor, insisting on the highest possible dividends, but as that of a friend who has been tied to India for centuries. After this brief span of time, the friend realizes a calling that he knows he must heed with the utmost earnestness, for India at present lies in great distress.

All the peoples of India have been deeply affected by Western science, Western techniques, indeed, by all of Western civilization. This has happened on our watch and under our direction. We built the railways, the cinemas, the schools, the colleges, we introduced our music, our literature, our clothes, our patterns of life. Inevitably, all of these pushed aside the indigenous culture and indigenous forms. Thus a revolution was begun over the entire, vast realm of life and thought in India. Due to the bond between us, India could not remain itself; by necessity, it became different from what it had been for a long time past. Of course, the influence on religion was extensive. Everywhere in the Far East, religion is the focus of civilization. All expressions of culture depend in one way or another on the religious view of the world; society is based upon it. When the forms of life and culture changed under the pressure of the Western world, religion could not remain unaffected and pristine. Religion itself was gripped by the same process of transformation. Great numbers of young people became disoriented; they no longer knew what to think, whom to pray to, whom to trust; they had lost their place. We bear a responsibility for all this, for it is we who led the Indian world into the enormous problems of modernity.

This fact alone should show us our spiritual calling toward the peoples that we ourselves have brought to so difficult a crisis. Indeed, we would be accountable if we did not help them to refind a spiritual hold, at fault if we did not support them in this confusion. We are called to guide the peoples of India through the darkness of these times.

We affirm that we shall be capable of doing so only when we put them in touch with the gospel. The gospel is the foundation of our own history. Our existence as a nation emerged from a struggle of faith. In the desperate days we have lived through, confronting the slogans of National Socialism with its glorification of race and its primordial Germanic paganism, we have seen more clearly than ever that only the gospel of Jesus Christ is our refuge. In prison and in misery, we have learned all over again to name the Name. When soon we face the peoples of India and enter upon a period of unity with them, spiritually we shall have nothing to utter other than His gospel. There is the place of safety and strength. There is our responsibility toward India. [. . .]

Het Parool. January 10, 1944

THIS IS HOW IT IS IN VUGHT

We happened upon a letter from Vught. A prisoner in that concentration camp secretly sent it. It says:

. . .

Chmiliefsky, the camp commandant, left the scene some time ago. He stole so much money, diamonds, and jewels from the Jewish prisoners that his loot must amount to many millions. It must have become obvious in Berlin that the yield of Jewish plunder transmitted by Chmiliefsky was suspiciously low. This led to the uncovering of his personal thefts.

Rheinecke, the subcommander, is also gone. Following the example of his chief, he too had enriched himself scandalously. Together with Chmiliefsky and some of the SS officers he held regular drinking bouts and orgies. Attractive young Jewish girls in the camp were picked out and forced to participate. Thereafter the SS scum raped them.

Etlinger, the substitute Schutzhaftlagerführer [commander for the policing of the camp], who amused himself by entering the barracks and firing at random, has also disappeared. So he will not be able to enact his plan to personally torture prisoners in the executioner's cages of the new prison that has been built in the center of the camp.

Sathoff, the second Rapportführer, seems to have left for the eastern front. His specialty was making prisoners crouch back and forth under the bunks. He will have to try that now somewhere with the Russians in the Pripet Marshes.

Rottenführer Drecksack [corporal bag of shit]—the name we had given to the little fat man who used to place the heel of his boot on your bare toes—is also gone. Shortly before his disappearance he went to some place in Tilburg to pay a bill for the camp administration. He spent the money on drink. Thereupon he tried to force the creditor to whom the money was owed to give him a receipt.

The Rottenführer, whom we call only by his nickname *"het kerstmannetje"* [little father Christmas] and who is known for having formerly beaten dozens to death in Amersfoort, is still here. He does not seem to get as much fun from this sort of thing anymore, for he no longer bothers anybody; obviously he too has begun to notice that Germany is no longer able to win the war. The other SS bandits as well have calmed down a bit.

In the meantime, new scoundrels have been sent to us to replace the ones who left. A certain Adam Grünewald is now the Kampcommandant. A couple of weeks ago, this fellow saw fit to rouse almost all 1,200 remaining Jewish men and women from their beds for a roll call. The wretches were robbed of their last possessions and clothes. They got instead dirty and torn underwear without buttons, and old convict clothes. The guards tore brassieres off the women. Each person got a little piece of bread, and then all were loaded on baggage wagons at the railway station of Vught, 60 people to a car. Each car was provided with one vessel of water and one empty can. When the wagons were full, they were shut, barred, and fixed with barbed wire. The transport was destined for Poland. In all likelihood, the train will be shunted off on a sidetrack for a week somewhere in Germany; this sort of thing is customary with such transports. Incomprehensible that Dutch railway men are collaborating in it.

When we hear news of how the "free" people "outside" comport themselves, people in my place, having spent a couple of years in prisons and camps, tend to turn sour. I have been told that the number of Dutch girls and women who are seen necking in public with Germans runs into the tens of thousands, and that there are thousands of births of German babies with Dutch mothers. If that is true, it is disgusting. And when newly imprisoned arrivals tell you that cinemas showing nothing but German propaganda are filled to the limit, you get the miserable feeling that your own people have left you in the lurch.

Nowadays there are some 6,000 prisoners here. Many of them are so-called *"Jodenbegunstigers"* [Dutch: "those favoring Jews"] or *Judenfreunde* [German: "friends of Jews"] — as the Krauts call them.

However, the vast majority, some good ones excepted, are really common parasites; for instance, for some 500 guilders a month perhaps they had taken a Jew into their home. When they get into trouble one way or the other and end up in the camp here, they tell anyone who wants to listen that they have become anti-Semites, that all Jews are crooks and extortionists. And that sort of rabble is counted for "the glory of Holland" . . .

Het Parool. February 5, 1944

Temporary scarcity of paper accounts for a limited edition of the present issue. One more reason to see to it that this paper is circulated widely!

We Must Persevere!

The Dead and the Martyred Exhort Us

Rage and loathing trade places before the outrageous acts the Germans have added to their list at the onset of this year. The "Dutch" press prints exclusively what pleases the Krauts, but know that in Groningen, Almelo, Leiden, Soest, and elsewhere, rows of innocent people have been put to death like dogs out of revenge for an attack on some traitor. The Germans no longer search for the actual agent of such attacks. Arbitrariness is their "law," terror their authority. In some instances, the order was issued that corpses must lie in the street for a day and a night—exemplifying the subtlety of Germanic taste . . . With compassion, we think of the survivors of the murdered and of the irreparable loss they have suffered as victims of Himmler's terror. They experience how in the paradise of National Socialism a human life counts for nothing. And yet, such a life is the shrine enclosing the lasting value of democracy.

[. . .] The explanation of all terror is the oppressor's anxiety. The war has almost run its course, and it is a lost cause for the German. On land, on the sea, and in the air, he maneuvers desperately in his defense, but the Russian advance, the bombardments of German cities, the safe arrival of Allied convoys, landings behind the German lines near Rome, and an invasion in the west are irresistible . . . The Führer himself posed the alternatives: *"Sieg"* [victory] or *"Untergang"* [defeat]. The chance of a *Sieg* is gone. Defeat is the only thing left. Soon increasing bombardments will pulverize German cities. In the near future more and more thousands of German men will die in vain, east, west, and south. Meanwhile Himmler's terror will rave on, furiously, more devastating than ever. And we, Dutchmen, can count on more hostages, more murders, more plunder, more pressure . . .

As soon as you feel discouraged, think of those who fell! Think of the still places, some yet unknown to us, that later will be as so many places of pilgrimage; they are the places where Dutchmen stood bravely for the last time, facing the firing squad. Think of the countrymen who suffered martyrdom in a concentration camp while you were comfortably resting. Think of the ones who lost everything, the destitute, the deported, those dragged away, the tortured, the mistreated, the dead. Their ranks are still growing. Every day, names are added to those of Amersfoort, Vught, Ommen, Westerbork, Dachau, Oranienburg, Buchenwald, and thousands of other of Hitler's places of terror. All these names, all these dead . . . signify for us . . . only one thing: the freedom we lost and which we shall regain, no matter what the cost. [. . .]

Reader, take care! When a Gestapo asks if you receive this or that illegal paper, possibly he already knows. In that case denial leads to unpleasantness. Better to affirm that you did receive it, and—it goes without saying—without reading you sacrificed it to your poor fuelless stove.

A TRANSPORT LEAVES

An Eyewitness Reports on the Sorrows and Strange Joys at Westerbork

After this night I honestly thought that it would be a sin ever to laugh again. But later it occurred to me that there were some who departed laughing. This time, however, very few laughed. Perhaps in Poland there occasionally may still be someone who laughs. There won't be many from this transport, I believe.

Early in the morning, after a night in the hospital barrack, I passed by the penal barracks . . . People stood by, mainly men, ready for the journey, behind barbed wire. Many looked almost stout, and enterprising. One old acquaintance I did not recognize under the shorn scalp that can transform people completely; he laughed and called out to me: "If they don't beat me to death at once, I'll come back!" But those babies, those little piercing cries of the babies that were picked up from their cribs in the middle of the night to be carried off to a distant land—. I must write all this down one thing after the other without stopping. Later I won't be able to do it, because I shall believe that it did not really happen. Even now it is like a mirage that floats away from me. The babies were the worst. And then that lame little girl who did not even want to take a dinner plate with her and who had such trouble with the thought of having to die. And that frightened boy: he had thought he was safe, and unexpectedly he too had to go. And he got into a mad fit and ran away. Fellow Jews had to hunt for him. If he had not been found, dozens of others would have to go on transport for him. They surrounded him soon enough. He was found in a tent, and *trotzdem—trotzdem* [German: "in spite of that"] the others had to go on transport too, by way of deterrent, it is called. In this way he dragged several good friends along with him. He caused fifty victims with that moment of mental derangement. Of course, he did not really do it. Our commander, of whom they often say that he is a gentleman, did it.

The previous afternoon, once more, I had walked through the hospital barrack, from bed to bed. Which [bed] would be empty tomorrow? Transport lists are not made known until the very last moment, and yet some already know beforehand that they have to leave. A young girl calls me, a girl with thin wrists and a transparent, small face. She is partly paralyzed, and she had just learned to begin walking again, between two nurses, a step at a time. "Did they tell you? I have to leave," she whispers. "What? Do you have to go?" We look at each other without speaking. Her face has disappeared altogether. She has only eyes. At last, she says in a monotonous, gray little voice: "And what a pity, eh, that now whatever you have learned in life—it has all been for nothing." And then she says: "How difficult it is, isn't it, to die, eh?"

In the laundry shed a disheveled little woman has a tray of dripping clothes on her arm. She grips my hand. She pours a stream of words over me. "It can't happen, can it? They are taking me away, and I can't even get my laundry dry before tomorrow. And my child is sick. A fever. Can't you see to it that I won't have to leave? I don't have enough clothes for the child. They sent me these tiny crawlers instead of the large ones—oh, I'm going out of my mind. And on the transport you can't take more than one blanket with you. We'll freeze to death, won't we?"

Little bottles of milk are prepared for the babies, whose pitiful cries penetrate every crevice of the barrack. A young mother says, almost apologetically: "Normally my child does not cry. It's just as if it knows what is going to happen." She picks up the child, a delightful baby of eight months, from its primitive crib and smiles at it: "If you aren't good, mommy won't take you with her on her travels!" She talks to me about acquaintances: "When the Grüne came to pick them up, the children cried terribly. Then the father said: 'Stop crying, for if you are not good now, you can't come along in the green car, and the green gentleman won't take you with him.' That did the trick, and the children calmed down." She winks courageously. She is a little, olive-dark woman, her face shows her sense of humor. She is dressed in long gray pants and a green woolen sweater. "I am laughing now, but I am not really so plucky," she says.

The woman of the wet laundry is close to insanity. "Can't you hide my child for me? Please, can't you put it away somewhere? He is running a fever—how can I take him with me?" She points to the little heap that is the child, with blond curls and a face of intense red, tossing in its rough wooden bed.

A few beds further, I suddenly see the ash-pale, freckled face of a colleague at the bed of a dying woman who has taken poison . . .

"God Almighty, what's happening, what are you doing?" (While I turn to the patient) the words slip out. She (the patient) is a working-class type from Rotterdam, petite, affectionate. She is in her ninth month. Two nurses are trying to dress her. Now she stands, leaning her misshapen body against the bed of one of her children. Sweat runs over her face. She gazes into a distance into which I cannot follow her, and she says in a toneless voice: "Two months ago, I wanted to go with my husband to Poland, and then I was not allowed to, because I always have such heavy labor. And now I have to leave—because this past night someone ran away—." The lament of the babies increases, it fills the nooks and crannies of the half-dark, sepulchral barrack. A name arises in my mind: Herod. On the stretcher, going to the train, labor sets in. That's why they are permitted to carry this woman back to the hospital instead of putting her on the cargo train. This night, this fact may be counted among the unfathomable human deeds.

I pass the lame girl's bed. With the help of others, she is already partly dressed. I have never seen such large eyes in such a small face. "I can't cope," she whispers. She stands before me, her green silken kimono wrapped around her deformed little figure. Her eyes are the eyes of a child, pure yet wise. She looks at me searchingly for a long time without a word, then she cries out passionately: "What I would like—oh, what I would like is to swim away in my tears to a better world!" Then: "And I am so terribly homesick for my good mother." (This good mother died of cancer in the camp, some months before, in the laundry shed near the toilet; in that place she could at least be alone for a moment, in order to die.)

You can tell that the young woman at one time was used to luxury, and that she was beautiful. She has not been long in the camp. She was in hiding, for the sake of her baby. Now she is here, because of betrayal, like so many of those who went into hiding. Her husband is in the penal barracks. She looks pitiful. With a greenish radiance, her own black hair shows here and there through the hair that is bleached. She is wearing several sets of underwear, although one cannot wear everything, especially when accompanied by a little child. As it is, she looks ridiculous . . . She glances at everyone with her eyes veiled and questioning, like a trapped young animal. Dilapidated now, what will this woman look like when after three days she is unloaded from a cargo wagon pushed full of men, women, children, babies, together with their baggage, and no furniture except in the center one can? Probably, other transition camps will be the next destination, from which other transports will leave. We are being hunted to death across Europe—.

It is six o'clock in the morning now. The train leaves at eleven. A beginning is made with loading the people and backpacks.

Men of the *Fliegende Kolonne* [the flying column] in brown overalls are bringing baggage on wheelbarrows. Among them I recognize a few of the commandant's court jesters: the comedian Max Ehrlich, and Willy Rosen the songwriter, who looks like a skeleton. A while back he was assigned to a transport, but several nights before he was to leave he was singing his lungs out in front of an audience, among which was the commandant with his entourage. He sang "Ich kann es nicht verstehen dasz die Rosen blühen" [German: "I cannot understand that the roses are blooming"] and other, similar *zeitgemässe* [in accordance with the time, "relevant"] songs. The commandant, who is so well educated in music, was delighted by the performance, and ordered Willy Rosen *gesperrt* [exempt from transport]. There is yet another court jester: Erich Ziegler, the commandant's favorite pianist. Legend has it that Erich Ziegler is such a virtuoso he can jazz up even Beethoven's Ninth Symphony. And surely, that means something.

From the looks of it, the freight carriages can be called full. That's what you would think. Good heavens, do all those people over there have to go inside as well? [. . .] Suddenly, a child calls out: "The commandant!" He appears at the beginning of the asphalt road, just like a famous star appearing on stage for the great finale of a revue. Legends are beginning to be woven around this commandant. He has so much charm, and he means so well for the Jews. Considering his position in life, he certainly does hold unusual ideas. Recently he decided we should have nutritional variety, and immediately we were given peas one day instead of cabbage. He is also the so-called father of our artistic life here. Occasionally he invites artists to his home; he talks and drinks with them. And the other evening he accompanied an actress to her barrack, and when saying good-night he shook her hand. Just imagine, shaking hands!

This morning he is sending 50 more Jews on transport, because a boy in blue pajamas hid in a tent. He trots alongside the train, his neatly brushed gray hair showing at the back of his head from under his flat, light green cap. Many ignorant teenagers here have a crush on that bit of gray hair contrasting so romantically with a rather young face, even though they would not say so publicly.

A number of Jewish big shots in camp life also parade alongside the train. "They try so hard to make themselves '*wichtig*' [important] too," someone behind me whispers. And I ask the companion next to me: "Will anybody ever be able to describe what is going on here?" Perhaps the outside world thinks of us only as a homogeneous gray mass of suffering Jews. Outsiders know nothing of the nuances and abysses, the fences between individuals here. They may never be able to understand it.

The light green, rigid commandant, the beige, immobile secretary, the black bully figure of the Oberdienstleiter [top chief of service] parade the length of the train. Everyone makes room for them; everyone turns their eyes toward them. Heavens, is it true that those doors finally close, completely? The doors are shut against the pile of people in the cargo carriages. Narrow openings near the top reveal heads, and later, when the train begins to move, they will show the waving hands. Once more, the commandant inspects the train, from beginning to end, this time on a bicycle. Then he gestures with his hand, just like a king in an operetta, and a little orderly rushes to him and respectfully receives the bicycle. The whistle makes its piercing sound, and a train with one thousand and twenty Jews leaves Holland; the twenty make up the reserve and serve to cover the risks of transport — .

News in Brief

Many residents are receiving questionnaires from the Amsterdam Records Office requesting data concerning civil status, etc. Keep in mind: this is an attempt to repair the destroyed Registry of Population. Whatever has been destroyed must remain destroyed! Put those papers into your stove. You did not receive anything!

Ons Volk [our people]. March 1944

A Living Democracy

Not long ago the institution of Democracy seemed to have perished ingloriously in the confrontation of nations. Some three years ago, many of us would have placed their bet a hundred to one on the dictators. But . . . the tide has turned . . .

It is no accident that Democracy is ascendant. What at first seemed to be her weakness turned out to be her strength . . . Not desiring war, she closed her eyes and did not want to see that Germany, Italy, and Japan had been preparing for war for years, spending the revenues of their nations on weaponry rather than butter. Yes, in the democracies there were statesmen who saw the danger, but what difference did they make so long as they could not convince anyone else? For here we have the essence of democracy. As long as a very large part of the people have not been won for a decision, those people cannot be moved. This is democracy's weakness, and also its strength, for whoever marches only because he is whipped will run away as soon as he has the chance . . .

[. . .] Many a critic carps when his democracy fails to appreciate that which he, the critic, considers important. But is it not a glory of democracy that the views of a minority cannot prevail? A dictator can ram down the throat of his people whatever he chooses, but how long can what has been rammed down be preserved? After all, what is truly important in the life of nations is not attained without an inner moral strength. The whip cannot create such strength . . .

[. . .] The [much criticized] parliamentary system has not often been allowed to work without obstruction. In Germany before the [First] World War, parliament was always confronted by the power of the king and the army, which was figuratively and literally its own army. Though the circumstances of England, France, and America were different, in those nations we have often found the parliamentary body opposed by foes who were no less powerful than kings: the great banks, and the great industrial and commercial enterprises. Sometimes those foes took refuge in bribes and coercion in order to redirect parliaments in their favor . . .

[. . .] Most certainly, even if material well-being and spiritual and moral freedom all were realized, even then humanity would not have attained paradise. Suffering would still exist, on account of sickness and death, on account of children who cause concern, on account of the great unknowns that would always stir us: the question of why we are here, the question of death, . . . the oppressive question of the Infinite. However, at that time [when real democracy has been realized] even the simplest among us will feel these concerns against a social background that is secure and just . . .

Invasion and German Fear

For weeks the newspapers have been filled with stories about the coming invasion. The Germans would like us to believe that at the very latest it will happen in March. Supposedly Churchill said at New Year's: "Within ninety days." This is a lie. Neither Churchill nor [Franklin Delano] Roosevelt has said anything of the sort.

Why do the Germans want us to believe that invasion will come in March, and not, for instance, in May or June?

Perhaps they are trying to gain heart themselves. They are frightened. Thus they want the German people to get used to the idea of an Allied landing in the near future. Of course, the propaganda adds that Germany is prepared and the landing will fail. Indeed they don't just say this, but scream it out. Every day they scream, like children afraid in the dark.

[. . .] The Germans are nervous. Which is understandable. Things are bad on the eastern front. They have fought there for more than two and a half years. Three months after it began they were told they had gained the victory. After nine months they had "almost" won. One more offensive, and the "Bolshevik hordes" would be annihilated. And now for months on end, they have been engaged in retreating victoriously. They score one defensive success after another. And the German statesmen no longer dare predict where it will end.

[. . .] It has all become too much for them: . . . more and more dead, more wounded and mutilated . . . It has been quite a while since the Germans gave up their hope of beating the Russians. But then, what? Is there no way out? Must the nation bleed to death?

There is a way out: the invasion. If the invasion is a failure, some newspapers write, the Germans will reinforce the eastern front with fresh troops. Then things will come to a quick end, and this hell will be over with. If only the invasion would come about soon— . . . it is the only hope for them, the only way out.

[. . .] We too hope for the invasion . . . But we do not want to rush it . . . We prefer the certainty that victory will come and will be complete.

Trouw. Mid-March 1944

The Inundations

The ever-expanding evacuation is disrupting our national existence more and more. First it was specific quarters of The Hague and other parts of the coast. Now, we have evacuations from still more regions that the Germans want to inundate. This is the most immediate — we would almost say: the most old-fashioned — war misery. Stripped of their livelihood, deprived of everything, people find themselves among strangers and without any prospect at all. Moreover, the inundation is a disaster in itself, especially when there is salt or brackish water, as in Zeeland and the islands of South Holland. Then the soil absorbs the salt, and as a result the land becomes useless for a long time, and grass and trees begin dying. [. . .]

News Items

[. . .] The inundation of islands in Zeeland and South Holland has led to the loss of 53 million kilograms of potatoes that were stored in pits, because of the lack of means of transportation.

[. . .] The Post, Telegraph, and Telephone Service has concluded a contract by which many employees are to be sent to Germany without delay for work in offices of the German State Mail.

In the past year, 4,000 pilots of the Allied forces have been buried in the Netherlands.

On the night of February 25–26 a group of twelve persons with masks made an attack on the police station of Delft. They took 35 revolvers and freed three prisoners.

W., March 30, 1944

Dear Johan and family,

Finally I am able to send you another few lines, in the hope that you will receive this epistle in good health. I have been hospitalized here for 3½ weeks now, with an ear infection, and I had surgery the day before yesterday. Fortunately, I feel good. How are things going with you? As you will notice, there is a special package stamp with this letter. You are permitted to mail a package of 2 kilos only with this stamp. It goes without saying that I'll be ever so grateful. The stamp has to be glued on the box, under the wrapping paper. I advise you not to send bread. Okay, now I have really nothing more to commandeer. How are the other families? Of course, my warm greetings go to all, also at school. How are Pietje and Kruina? Do they still go to school? Well, friends, I am finishing with warm greetings, the very best, and so long, your Ben

> Absender: Benj. Wessels
> Baracke: 3 Saal E geboren: 28-9-'26
> LAGER WESTERBORK

Ons Volk. April 1944

Stienus Bertus Van Wijnen

In January, police lieutenant A. J. Elzinga was shot to death in Groningen. The Germans took countermeasures . . . Innocent Dutchmen were murdered. And they were innocent indeed, for these people were unaware of the shooting. They were murdered by Germans? Yes, but also by "Dutchmen."

Stienus Bertus van Wijnen is one of those . . . It was [he] who shot Mr. Zigterman and Mr. Bossinga, residing in the Ebbingestraat in Groningen . . .

Van Wijnen still serves as captain of the police force in [the city of] Meppel. With this report we print the picture of this murderer.

Trouw. Mid-April 1944

APRIL 30. THE BIRTHDAY OF THE PRINCESS

We mark the fourth birthday Princess Juliana is to celebrate on foreign soil. [Queen Wilhelmina resided in England during the occupation.] It seems so very long ago that she was in our midst, and we could share in her joy as a young wife and mother. The princess' birthday was the last of the royal festivities that we were able to experience in happiness with her.

[. . .] On this, the thirtieth of April we offer respectful and heartfelt congratulations to our beloved princess, her royal mother, the prince consort, and the three little princesses. God willing, au revoir, soon.

THE JEWISH PROBLEM

[This article is in some ways a repetition of an Oct. 30, 1943, article in *Het Parool.* Its particular importance at this later date, and the shift in perspective it shows justify a full translation nevertheless.]

Until the moment when the steamroller of German Nazism rode into Holland, no Jewish problem existed within our borders. Here Jews were peaceful citizens who made their living each in his own way. In some trades Jews gave sharp competition to the Christians, but on the whole this created no conflict. Most Jews had assimilated themselves; a smaller group held faithfully to the Jewish tradition and in so doing more or less isolated itself. None of this led to clashes or disagreeable tensions.

The political sympathies of Jews were distributed among the parties on the left. Certainly, for our country the fable that Jews always have a hand in revolutionary stirrings simply won't wash. We had

Jewish communists, but also Jewish old liberals; there were even Jews with antirevolutionary inclinations. [The political party officially known as the Anti-Revolutionary Party formed the backbone of *Trouw.*] In any event, the idea that Jews ever called the tune in politics is out of the question. Jewish ministers [in government] were exceptional, as were Jewish mayors. On the whole, Jews enjoyed the favor of the whole populace, especially in the lower ranks of society. This fact was shown most emphatically in Amsterdam in the great strike of February 25, 1941.

Anti-Semitism of the sort known in other countries barely existed here . . . The change came about after May 1940. The Nazis succeeded in shoving their Jewish problem down our throats. We were never sufficiently on guard. In the beginning, we were naive. It seemed that for the time being we did not need to worry about the measures aimed at Jews and intending to separate the Jewish part of the nation from the rest. Many, almost all, public servants signed the . . . Aryan declaration [a form stating that the undersigned was not Jewish]. The Jews themselves reported as Jews en masse and were thus led as sheep to their slaughter. All of us cooperated in the complete registration and without protest picked up our *persoonsbewijs* [personal identity card imposed by the Germans]. We came to our senses and realized the danger only when it was too late. Then we tried to save what could be saved, and stretched out the hand of compassion to those we should have defended much sooner.

Now that the fact is accomplished, and virtually no Jews are present in our land, we are bewildered that we have allowed this to happen. We lived by the morality of Cain: "Am I my brother's keeper?" We had forgotten that the injustice done to others is also our concern. We did not see that compassion is no substitute for the preservation of justice. We certainly wished to help, but after the manner of a man who remains secure on dry land while putting out his hand to one who is drowning.

In somewhat the same lopsided manner, there has resulted from all this the mistaken idea that in our country a Jewish problem has come to exist . . . If we are not careful, we shall be stuck after the war with a Jewish problem that . . . will play havoc with us psychologically . . . Many nowadays look upon the Jew as a different being, distinguished from the other Dutch citizens, a being whom we in our kindness are to take under our protection. Then, if among our protégés some turn out not to be worthy of our favors, or worse, if under duress they betray us, we easily swing into anti-Semitism, and thus fall into line with National Socialism.

Hence it is essential that we reflect very seriously on what relation we find ourselves in vis-à-vis the Old People. First, something about the disappointments many of us have experienced in our preoccupations with Jews. It has been observed before that everything Jewish is under one and the same threat, and that among Jews who are in hiding there are certainly to be found some weak, nervous, egoistic, dishonest, and inferior characters. On the other hand, we may assume that those non-Jews who went into hiding must be on the whole among the best specimens, the most courageous, the most daring, the ones who are willing to sacrifice. Among non-Jews, the scum of society separated itself from danger; only think of the conduct of the Dutch SS and the W.A. at arrests and in concentration camps . . . With the Jews no such separation could occur. Moreover, for each bad behavior of a Jew we can at once point to another who behaved well indeed, or to some low exploitation and thievery by so-called Christians who saw fit to abuse the dependent position of Jews. No, we non-Jews have no reason at all to think that we would acquit ourselves any differently than our Jewish friends under the same circumstances.

But this still does not reach the core of the problem. We shall be able to bear any disappointment from Jews or non-Jews more adequately if we see that all we do is a necessary part of our Christian duty. We ought to help the Jews not because we feel sorry for them in their persecution, but because this persecution is an assault on God's justice. Every persecution militates against the Divine commandment of love for the neighbor.

The oppression of the Jews should concern us most especially because it arises in principle from a heathenish hatred of all that is reminiscent of Almighty God. The fact that God chose ancient Israel as the people of His covenant and out of it brought forth the Savior is now the ground for the fanatic insanity that seeks the extinction of this people. And for us this same fact is the point of departure for indefatigable efforts to strengthen and support, despite all disappointments.

What takes place once again in our day shows that no man and no people can call God's curse over itself with impunity. At the cross of Golgotha the reckless words were heard: "Let His blood come over us and our children!" [. . .]

Moreover, the consequences of Israel's deepest fall must not be a criterion for our behavior. Let us not involve ourselves in God's judgment, so that we do not fall under that same judgment. What holds true for us is only this, that we should see in the Jew God's creature, which fell into sin with us, but for whose salvation Christ died on the cross.

If we stand thus before the Jewish people, every trace of anti-Semitism will depart from us. Then, for the future, we shall regard the Jews as fellow citizens, with the same rights, and more than this, we shall do everything we can to wipe out the abuse and indignity of these years, which will certainly have brought about unfathomable psychic injury among the Jews themselves.

Het Parool. April 26, 1944

He Was Lucky!

Somewhere in the Netherlands, three officials of the Sicherheitsdienst [Security Service] boarded a train and began their checking of *persoonsbewijzen* [identity cards]. A young man whose age made him a candidate for the *Arbeitseinsatz* [forced labor in Germany] became very nervous. A policeman who sat opposite him understood the situation and pulled out a pair of handcuffs and put them on the boy's wrists. When the Germans came along and saw that the young man was a detainee, they did not ask him anything and left him alone. Just before the next station, the constable loosened the handcuffs, saying: "*Onderduikers* [people in hiding from the Germans] do not belong on the train. Get out of here." Thus he let him go. With joy and gratitude we establish the fact that the Netherlands still has such policemen!

[The following postcard is written in German:]

May 7, 1944

Dear Johan,

Fortunately, I can tell you that I am in excellent shape. A food package would please me a great deal, and also please some wool for mending. Warm regards also for your parents and sisters.

Ben

Absender: Benj. Wessels 28/9-'26
Aufenthaltslager
Bergen-Belsen (bei Celle)
Baracke 16
reply only on
postcards in the German language

Ons Volk. May 1944

MESSAGE OF HER MAJESTY THE QUEEN

Fellow Countrymen,

In the past I have often addressed you by radio. Now that in these unparalleled times I am given the chance to communicate with you through the secret press, I do not want to leave this extraordinary instrument unused. For indeed, we should make use of everything that can contribute to our unity.

From your courageous underground press and from other sources, I learn how in these difficult days you are surviving and struggling. The living voice of the *Engelandvaarders* [general term for all who risked their lives to escape the occupied country and sailed to England] furthers my understanding even more. They witness to your suffering, your struggle, and the hope you bear. Above all, they witness to your unshakable faith in victory, which is the foundation of your courage . . . in adversity. Know that you are not alone. We are fighting side by side for the truth, for justice, for liberation.

We are fighting for the sake of the pure, new nation of the Netherlands that must be born from this war, of which you now feel the misery and the pain, but that with God's help shall arise.

[Signed:] WILHELMINA

WHAT DID NOT APPEAR IN NEWSPAPERS [THE OFFICIAL, OR LEGAL, PAPERS]:

[. . .] "That will not happen to me," the National Socialist mayor of IJsselstein said, two days before his own rationing office was attacked. Hence, together with a pal, he personally watched over the safe. The attackers gave him the opportunity to see the safe from the inside for a change, while for a good purpose 9,000 rationing coupons were set free . . .

[. . .] Max Blokzijl [an active Dutch Nazi who had become head of the Department of the Press; executed in 1946] announced an amnesty for *onderduikers*. The only thing (!) *onderduikers* are expected to do is report to the Germans and offer their services for a "useful and positive purpose." On this basis an *onderduiker* in the province of Groningen did report to the Germans. Three days later he was dead. He was interrogated by the Grüne Polizei. In all likelihood the young man did not want to betray his host. [. . .]

IN CASE OF INVASION:

1. Remain quiet and do not cause any hindrance to our Allies.
2. Take precautions in order to get through a time of stress as well as possible.
3. Do not help the enemy.
4. If possible, provide help to the Allied forces.

IN MEMORIAM

From time to time the [official] papers report the names of underground fighters . . . who are mowed down by the enemy's firing squads. We all know that more executions take place than the newspapers speak of.

Thus, on April 14, eight courageous young men met their deaths. Their stand was a profession of faith that characterizes the resistance group to which they belonged, and we wish here to honor their memory. In them we revere all whose names are as yet unmentioned but are inscribed in the book of our time. These heroes willingly gave their lives for the sake of the country. The process against the so-called group of Meppel took place in The Hague. The young men knew beforehand that after the verdict they would be shot within twenty-four hours. The hatches of their cells were kept open and the lights remained on all night. During this night they could write a last letter home.

Early in the night they began to sing: "A Mighty Fortress Is Our God." First softly, until others joined in, and then when there came the words "Let goods and kindred go, / This mortal life also," the song rang loud and clear throughout the jail, as if these eight already stood in exultation before God's throne. A wave of emotion engulfed the whole prison.

Thereupon, together they read, aloud, so that others could hear it, Psalms 42, 91, and, we are told, also Psalm 118. For almost the whole night, they exchanged psalms and songs, "The Lord is my shepherd," "Don't live your life alone," "A cheering tone," "I want to give Thee, God, my thanks."

By morning they prayed, and it seemed to the other prisoners as if they had already entered the home of their Lord and Savior. The grace these men received at their hour of death was overwhelming. Those who heard it understood what it means to expect everything from Jesus.

The Germans did not stop them. In the morning they were picked up. Following the example of the holy apostle Paul and Silas, they spent the last night of their young lives in prison singing songs. Endowed with faith and courage they entered a better, heavenly fatherland.

Thus died our young men, maligned as terrorists by the enemy. Our nation honors them as heroes and martyrs, whose blood will not have flowed in vain for the cause of justice and freedom.

[FROM THE LEGAL PRESS. At this point I enter a few items from the official, "legal" press, which continued to publish in the Netherlands during the war. The *Nieuwe Brielsche Courant,* a regional paper, was and still is published in Brielle, the principal city on the island of Voorne, four miles from Oostvoorne. After June 1943, scarcity of paper reduced it from its former two issues to one issue per week, and to a mere four pages. The issue dated June 9, 1944, reporting on the invasion, states that on June 6 paratroopers landed near the mouths of the Seine and Orne. The issue of June 16 reports that Mussert, the leader of the Dutch National Socialists, officially declared that he will put on his Wehrmacht uniform if the invasion reaches the Netherlands.]

Het Parool. June 19, 1944

THE INVASION HAS BEGUN!

Freedom Is Approaching. Be Prepared!

We were moved and delighted by the report on June 6 that Allied soldiers have begun the attack on Hitler's fortress. We waited for this day during four long and gruesome years. For four years we lived in darkness, within impenetrable walls. Like victims of a mine disaster, we had to wait until help came from outside.

[. . .] German tyranny has still to reach its zenith. At any price, the Germans must keep us from rendering aid to our Allies. They know that in every occupied region they are surrounded by hate and loathing, which at the right moment will be triggered into mass action. At any price, they will try to make us fear the consequences of such action . . .

What Can We Do?

[. . .] Unlike the Nazis, we do not fight out of an addiction to killing and destroying . . . [And furthermore,] we fight with unfortunately limited means. Our strategy must be adapted to those means, and we must avoid unnecessary sacrifices. This is the sense of General [Dwight D.] Eisenhower's message and [Dutch government-in-exile Prime] Minister [Pieter Sjoerds] Gerbrandy's speech on the first day of the invasion. Do not commit acts of resistance in public as yet, the Allied Supreme Command advised us. Wait for the moment to be right . . . When . . . our country has regained control, and as soon as we receive a clear sign from the Allies, we can begin the attack on the Germans from behind the front. Only this strategy will accelerate the victory to come.

Of course, Eisenhower's advice should not be used as an excuse for cowards to sneak off and desert the rest of us . . .

[FROM THE LEGAL PRESS. The *Nieuwe Brielsche Courant* of June 23, 1944, reports: "This past week Germany has mobilized its new attack weapon: planes without pilots." What is meant is the V-1 and V-2 missiles of the Wehrmacht (army) and the Luftwaffe (air force), respectively. See below, "News sheet without a title, December 1, 1944."

Nieuwe Brielsche Courant. July 7, 1944

In military circles in Berlin the state of affairs in the first month of the invasion of the Normandy coast has been sketched out. American and English forces were able to occupy only 5,200 km², i.e., only 1 percent of French territory.]

STILL: MY MAYOR

Once again, I think back to my pride in my mayor in former days. What a Dutchman he was! I remember his warm words, spoken at the right time. How he saddened me when he did so many things that I could never understand. Truly, he should have ceased to be my mayor! But still he is.

And now he is really going too far.

He called fellow citizens of mine to work on an airport, so that the enemy's air base can be readied in time. Their opponent will be our own army. Fortunately I am *ondergedoken* [in hiding], for otherwise he would certainly have called upon me too. I would have refused, and then my own mayor would have borne the guilt as concentration camp gates opened for me.

He has also executed his assignment of setting up poles to prevent paratroopers from landing. He put all my fellow citizens to work, and they set up thousands of poles on my village grounds, maintaining all the while that they had not done anything at all. The poles have been provided with neatly cut points, so that our Dutch boys when they come down might reach their fate in one fell swoop. Imagine remaining seated unharmed on such a disagreeable pole!

My mayor saw to it that alongside village roads, hideaway holes were dug, in which Germans can find cover when they operate against the advancing liberators. He took this care so that soon the enemy will be able to protect himself more easily while he kills our own men.

Moreover, my mayor turned others into accomplices. When somehow he began to feel that one thing and the other were really not in accord with the task Her Majesty the Queen, before whom he took his oath of office, had entrusted to him, he convened the dignitaries of the community—for the German rule entitled him to call up advisers. He presented them with the dilemma of what he ought to do. And because these dignitaries appreciated my mayor so, they said that one thing and the other were indeed very difficult—but we had better go ahead and do one thing and the other, for otherwise we might get an N.S.B.-er [as mayor in his place]. In this way, my mayor pulled my minister, my trustee, my banker, and many others with him into the conspiracy.

Oh what has become of my mayor — .

I still think back with nostalgia to the time when he was so very different. At that time I could trust him and count on him in all things. Nowadays he executes every German order. He has no more spine. How I remember his patriotic speeches at the occasion of the queen's birthday! My heart still warms when I think back on it. In fact, I grow hot and I tremble.

Would my mayor give such speeches again when the queen returns?

That depends on whether by then my mayor is still my mayor.

In case he is, I'll see fit to prevent him from speaking.

[FROM THE LEGAL PRESS. The *Nieuwe Brielsche Courant* of Friday, July 21, 1944, reports that the Wehrmacht commander for the west, General Field Marshal Hans Günter von Kluge, has spoken vehemently to German war correspondents, saying that he and General (Erwin) Rommel (who was von Kluge's comrade in arms) will stop at nothing to settle their score with their old foes, the English and Americans, whom they fought in the First World War.

The front at that moment was still in Normandy. Ironically, the same paper mentions, without details, the attempt on Hitler's life, in which Rommel had an important part and which took place the day before. Under the headline "Attempt on the Führer's Life," it relates that Hitler "got only light burns, that he returned to his work, and that he received the duce in conformity with his agenda."]

Het Dagelijks Nieuws [the daily news; published
in Leiden; second year of publication]. July 25, 1944

[. . .] Himmler has initiated a mop-up action that goes well beyond the carnage of June 30, 1934 . . . A great number of civil and military authorities have been imprisoned and executed, in Germany and in the occupied territories. The names of the generals who were shot are kept secret. In Berlin tanks are still rolling through the streets, and the clashes between SS and troops of the Wehrmacht continue. In several large cities in Germany machine guns have been set up on street corners.

The German borders are still hermetically closed, and hence reports that filter through are confused.

Hitler has ordered the ordinary military salute abolished for the entire army. From now on military men will greet each other with the Germanic salute.

Churchill returned to England from a three-day visit to France. He addressed members of the Royal Air Force at an airport in Normandy. He declared that Germany shows serious signs of weakness. The country is in a state of revolt; Germans are shooting at each other. In this context, he deemed it possible that the war in the west will come to an end soon.

RUSSIA

Once again there is excellent news from Russia. The Red Army is advancing very quickly toward the heart of Germany. [. . .]

ITALY

The Fifth Army conquered five cities in the plain of the Arno . . .

FRANCE

Except for local skirmishes, the Normandy front has never been as quiet as it is now. It would seem that this is the calm before the storm.

[FROM THE LEGAL PRESS. Reporting on the response to the assassination attempt on Hitler and the introduction of the Nazi salute for the entire army, the *Nieuwe Brielsche Courant* of July 28, 1944, reports that this "is the simple yet eloquent and proud response of the National Socialist Wehrmacht to the enemies of the Reich and to the saboteurs of Germany's decisive struggle."]

[An undated draft of a letter by Johan Schipper to the Jewish Council for Amsterdam:]

M.

Please let me know whether you can provide information concerning the family Wessels, previously living in Oostvoorne, Stationsweg.

N. B. Wessels, born in Oostvoorne April 19, 1922, was taken away in Aug. of 1942; nothing has been heard from him since.

Mr. I. Wessels, born . . . , and

Mrs. Wessels–van Dijk, born . . .

B. L. Wessels, born Sept. 28, 1926

were transported in Oct. 1942 to Amsterdam, and lived there

Plantage Franselaan 34, and

Weesperplein 1.

In September 1943, Mr. and Mrs. Wessels were transported to Westerbork and subsequently put on a transport to Poland, both serving as nurses.

B. L. Wessels was transported to Westerbork in Sept. 1943 and stayed there until April 1944, was then taken to G[ermany]. In May 1944 he sent me a postcard from Aufenthaltslager Bergen-Belsen (bei Celle), Baracke 16. Since then, I have not received word from him.

Sincerely yours,

— — —

[The subsequent answer is a form letter:]
JEWISH COUNCIL FOR
AMSTERDAM
DEPT. EXPOSITUR
Telephone 95248, 26274 8.8.44
Postal Account 447336 Amsterdam-Z.,
Jan van Eyckstraat 15
In replying, mention reference:
Mr. J. Schipper
Oostvoorne

Sir:

In answer to your letter of 8-5-'44 we inform you that we have not received any report from the persons you mention.

Correspondence can be carried on with those who are employed in Germany (Upper Silesia) and who have themselves initiated the correspondence, including persons in the camps at Bergen-Belsen (Kreis Celle, Germany) and Theresienstadt (Protektorat Böhmen-Mähren), in German and on postcards provided by the senders themselves and delivered by them to the post office.

Packages to Bergen-Belsen and Theresienstadt can be sent by mail or with the shipping firm Van Gend & Loos. As to victuals, one weekly rationing of rationed articles is permissible for shipment. In accordance with the rules of the camps, packages to Bergen-Belsen must not weigh more than 1 kg. It is also advisable not to exceed 2 kg. for packages to Theresienstadt. We have no information concerning packages to work camps.

Cash remittance is permitted only to Bergen-Belsen. According to the information known to us, one is permitted to send a monthly amount of RM.50 per person in the care of the canteen administration.

All transmissions are to take place by ordinary mail service. Registered dispatches, or shipments provided with "red cards" for confirmation of receipt are not permitted. From Theresienstadt, after a while one does receive personally signed confirmations of receipt.

Sincerely yours,

Röttgen

INFORMATION AND DOCUMENTATION

Immediately upon liberation, even before anything can be done about repatriation, the recovery and restoration of our fellow Dutchmen who went into hiding will require our fullest attention. In this respect, the condition of our Jewish fellow countrymen is more difficult than that of many others, because their families were ripped apart and no home awaits them. A far from easy task for our nation will be to watch over a proper channeling of the needed assistance.

[. . .] In addition to registration, this assistance will need to comprise housing, financial support, reschooling, training, legal help, governance of affairs for those who are still absent, etc.

[Title of publication missing] End of
September or beginning of October 1944

His Royal Highness Prince Bernhardt, the commander-in-chief of the Dutch Domestic Forces [the coordinated underground resistance groups in the Netherlands in wartime] addressed a communiqué to the people of the Netherlands, in which he says:

"When Allied troops liberate Dutch territory, the population is most emphatically advised not to show its joy by throwing flowers or fruit to the military. Enemies and treacherous elements have seen fit to hide explosives in flowers and fruit. As a result in some regions the Allied troops were forced to open fire on civilians. We trust that the people will express their joy in a way that is not open to misinterpretation."

Alles Sal Reg Kom ["everything will come out all right," a South
African adage well known in the Netherlands]. Oct. 20, 1944

Read and pass on quickly, for in the present circumstances most people are starved for news.

Western Front

Canadian troops entered Breskens and took 500 prisoners. In this sector a total of 3,000 prisoners have been taken.

Alles Sal Reg Kom. October 23, 1944

Read and pass on quickly, for in the present circumstances most people are starved for news.

Western Front

After conquering the town of Esschen in Belgium, Canadian troops reached the Dutch border. They are now 8 km from Roosendaal.

A new warning has been given to the large cities of the Netherlands to be on guard against *razzias,* for this is the means by which the Germans would like to eliminate the underground resistance groups.

[News sheet without a title]
December 1, 1944

Some Details Concerning the Propaganda Bomb

The V-1 weapon has been in operation against London for eighty days. In this period 8,000 flying bombs have been launched. Of this number 29%, or 2,300, have hit London; 25% were lost, and antiaircraft guns were able to destroy 46%. The V-1 offensive reached its climax on August 28, when 101 flying bombs were launched; no less than 97 were destroyed, so that on that day only four specimens reached their destination. During forty days of the V-1 period, on the average one person per bomb was killed; later on, this became one person for every three bombs. One can hardly attribute military significance to the flying bombs, as 72 of them came down on civilian quarters.

German V-1 propaganda has painted enormous ravages on London caused by the flying bombs. If we realize that one of these bombs contains approximately one ton of explosives, we see that during almost three months, 2,300 tons of explosives hit London. However, in one night the Royal Air Force dropped more than 3,000 tons on Germany, and not infrequently 12,000 tons are dropped on German land during a 24-hour period. [. . .]

[Title of publication missing]
December 1[?], 1944

The German propaganda machine just isn't what it used to be. Recently, the Germans shot pamphlets toward the American ranks. The text was in Russian and read: "The Americans are poised to attack Russia in the Pacific. Only a strong Germany can save Russia." A few hours later the geniuses "corrected" their mistake, and thus the Americans received sheets with an English text declaring: "Russia tries to destroy England and America . . ."

Het Aambeeld ["the anvil," stenciled in
Leeuwarden, Friesland]. April 14, 1945

THE FINAL ROUND

As we write these lines, the latest reports are reaching us. We learn, among other things, that our liberators are already on territory of the province of Friesland. The front is only a few dozen kilometers from us. [. . .]

Let all of us pray to God and place our trust only in Him for the outcome in the coming hours.

Let us turn to our Mother Mary and implore Her for Her help in the Frisian lands.

De Kieuwelander [published for Poortugaal—some 20 miles from Oostvoorne, and near Rotterdam—and environs; it is important to note that the following article appeared in a part of the Netherlands that was still under German control (definitive date of liberation for the whole country was to be May 5)]. April 22[?], 1945.

Buchenwald: the Other Germany

In the course of a few days, the Allied troops took possession of several German concentration camps. In one they found 60,000, and in the others 20,000 and 21,000 political prisoners. Journalists wired their reports from those camps to the rest of the world. The world press is outraged over what was discovered. General Eisenhower asked Churchill to send a committee of parliamentarians to the camps. Today this committee, consisting of ten members from the House of Lords and House of Commons (among them two physicians), began their journey. In answer to a question from a member of the Upper House, Churchill replied that England will make a case for punishment of the criminals who committed their crimes against German citizens.

The American commander of the city of Weimar has caused a thousand German residents to be taken, in groups of one hundred, to the nearby camp of Buchenwald in order to see what took place in their immediate vicinity. It is difficult to render in words what these visitors saw. They will be witnesses in a court of justice before which the guilty ones will have to respond.

Literally mountains of corpses and parts of corpses. Heaps of the bones of men and women . . . at the crematorium. Thousands and tens of thousands were slaughtered. In one of the buildings, a test station for experiments on human beings. Vivisection was practiced there . . .

So far as to the dead.

Are there still some alive in these camps?

Yes. Living corpses, skeletons. Usually they are too weak to walk. In rows of three above each other, neglected, filthy, they lie on boards. Of the 100,000 who were found alive in the three camps, 20,000 are in critical condition. Thousands of cases of typhus and typhoid fever. In addition, dysentery and other contagious diseases.

For some days now endeavors are made at Buchenwald to get 21,000 people to the point where they can digest normal food without risking their lives . . . And this concerns "the healthy ones." Some forty prisoners are dying every day; for them salvation came too late . . .

There are 900 children in the concentration camp of Buchenwald, mostly orphans. Their parents, imprisoned like them, have been murdered or dragged off. The youngest child is two years old. Prisoners considered these children their common possession, for whom they were responsible. The American physicians were struck by the fact that the physical condition of the children was better than that of the adults. Prisoners gave from their own rations to the children, although they were famished themselves. They did what they could in the circumstances. In spite of that, the children, with their childish bodies, have the faces of old people.

[. . .] We lack the words, both for the misery and suffering, and for the bestiality.

In this way Germans have suffered at the hands of Germans . . .

Is there another Germany nevertheless?

We are only acquainted with *moffen* [the Dutch derogatory term for Germans; stronger than "Kraut," which here especially would be too weak a rendering].

Is it worth the trouble to speak of that other Germany? Can we distinguish between Germans and *moffen*? We think that we can. People who knew how to bear an unbearable burden for the sake of their conviction, people who were able in the midst of such misery to keep their humanity alive, are entitled to our attention . . .

The world is full of hate for the *moffen*, and understandably so.

The world demands justice; the world demands reparation of injustice to the very limits of the German nation's strength. And understandably so.

Under the dominating feelings of hatred, the duty of conscience to distinguish between German and *mof* becomes vague. It is troublesome to make the distinction. But it is unreasonable not to make it. Let us turn for a moment to the people of the Netherlands.

When the Germans still seemed to be rulers of western Europe, they were able to win over quite a few Dutchmen for well-paid work in the Organisation Todt [German industrial enterprise that occupied itself with the building of German fortifications], and hardly under duress! Thousands of Dutchmen have taken part in building fortifications along the French coast. Frenchmen despised them. They used a strong term for those Dutchmen: *les boches du Nord,* or in Dutch: *de moffen van het Noorden* [the Krauts from the north]. Many a Dutchman would beat any Frenchman who called him that. There are Dutchmen who deserve this judgment nevertheless. And yet, the same judgment, if used against one and all, is untenable.

This example concerns how a people is seen from abroad. But isn't there a much sharper example within our nation itself? We have had to learn many lessons in the last five years. The most important, which we may ignore only at the peril of more misery, is this: the separation of the wheat from the chaff did not present a neat line between confessions of faith, nor between parties, nor between social groups. The separation between the courageous and the cowardly, between men with and without character, between witnesses with deeds and witnesses only with words, runs right through the confessions, the parties, the social groups. Not one among us—if for this exceptional occasion we may generalize in the midst of our most diverse readership—has not been disappointed during these years in his trust in a member of his own confessional, political, or social circle. No one among us has not at one time or another watched with respect the model presented by some person of another circle—one whom he had never seen before the war except as an opponent. And if some among us have disappointed ourselves—for this too has happened—may it not have been forgivable?

In view of these experiences within our own nation and in our own bosom, we are obliged to apply these bothersome, yet reasonably required distinctions also to the Germans. We know the objection that arises now: "The Germans who were Germans and who resisted the *moffen* were so few." And further: "What became of their resistance?"

Let us respond. These words reproach the victims of Buchenwald. The piled up corpses can no longer speak. But someone can speak for them; to that they are entitled. It should be an intercessor who has earned the right to speak for them, because among the victims of the beasts of Buchenwald he has friends. He worked with them within and outside of Germany. They are the ones whose remains were burned in the ovens of Buchenwald because they resisted Hitler, because they wanted to save Europe from the destruction Hitler's system had in store for it. They were this way because they were Germans, and not *moffen*. They wished to be Europeans, not "Teutons." And that is how they were, long before the war. They were thus at the time when [former Dutch prime minister Hendrikus] Colijn said [before the war] that "the Netherlands could go to sleep in peace."

Who then are those victims of the human-shaped plague that came over us? They were the best from all circles and groups of German society. Not hundreds, but thousands of workers of the Social Democratic and Communist Parties and of the labor unions, thousands of ministers and priests, monks and nuns. They were as well members of free-spirited, liberal, democratic parties and of the middle classes.

I W

INFORMATION WORK

OF THE DUTCH ISRAELITIC CONGREGATION IN UTRECHT

Utrecht (Holland), November 11, 1945

Mrs. [sic] J. W. Schipper
Oostvoorne, Z. H.
Hevering B327

Dear Mrs. Schipper,

Ref. W 449/452

In reply to your letter of November 4, we inform you that until this moment no information has reached us concerning

Nathan Benjamin Wessels

I. Wessels

A. Wessels–van Dijk.

We placed the names of the persons mentioned in our search file and we shall report to you as soon as we have received any news.

Concerning Benjamin Leo Wessels we regret to inform you that he died in Bergen Belsen on March 22, 1945.

Sincerely yours,

I.W.
Information Work N.I.G.
Utrecht
Dr. Landsberger

THE DUTCH RED CROSS OFFICE FOR THE LIQUIDATION
OF CONCENTRATION CAMPS S/AV. 's-GRAVENHAGE, Dec. 15, 1945
Burnierstraat 1
Telephone 110697
Department of Jewish Investigation
No. 7617 W 449/451

Subject:

Enclosures:

In reply, mention Dept. and number.

Mr. J. W. Schipper
I. bevering [sic]
B327
Oostvoorne (Z.H.)

In answer to your request, we inform you that Mr. Nathan Benjamin Wessels, born 4/19/22
was deported from Westerbork for an unknown destination,
Izaak Wessels, born 9/29/86, and
Antje Wessels–van Dijk, born 10/25/87
were deported from Westerbork to Auschwitz. Further information is not available.

The Chief of the Office for the
Liquidation of Concentration Camps.

signed for him,

K. Selowsky

Index

Kees W. Bolle, a professor emeritus of history at UCLA, is a
historian of religions. He has a special interest in India and Sanskrit
(*The Bhagavadgītā: A New Translation*, 1979), as well as in the widespread problem of *mis*understanding religious matters, the nature
of secularization processes, and the striking function of humor in
religious traditions (*The Freedom of Man and Myth*, 1993). He is the
general editor of "Hermeneutics: Studies in the History of
Religions," an ongoing monograph series (1973–).